MW00424241

# THE ANCIENT EIGHT

## Also by John Feinstein

*Feherty*

*Raise a Fist, Take a Knee*

*The Back Roads to March*

*The First Major*

*The Legends Club*

*Where Nobody Knows Your Name*

*One on One*

*Moment of Glory*

*Are You Kidding Me!*

*Living on the Black*

*Tales from Q School*

*Last Dance*

*Next Man Up*

*The Classic Palmer*

*Let Me Tell You a Story*

*Caddy for Life*

*The Punch*

*Open*

*The Last Amateurs*

*The Majors*

*A March to Madness*

*The First Coming*

*A Civil War*

*Winter Games*

*A Good Walk Spoiled*

*Play Ball*

*Running Mates*

*Hard Courts*

*Forever's Team*

*A Season Inside*

*A Season on the Brink*

# THE ANCIENT EIGHT

## College Football's Ivy League and the Game They Play Today

JOHN FEINSTEIN

*New York*

Jacket design by Terri Sirma
Jacket images: left © matscisteph/Shutterstock; right © Thomas M Perkins/Shutterstock; texture © MM_photos/Shutterstock
Jacket copyright © 2024 by Hachette Book Group, Inc.



Hachette Books
Hachette Book Group
1290 Avenue of the Americas
New York, NY 10104
HachetteBooks.com
Twitter.com/HachetteBooks
Instagram.com/HachetteBooks

First Edition: November 2024

Published by Hachette Books, an imprint of Hachette Book Group, Inc.
The Hachette Books name and logo is a trademark of the Hachette Book Group.



Library of Congress Control Number: 2024943672

ISBNs: 978-0-306-83390-8 (hardcover), 978-0-306-83392-2 (ebook)

Printed in Canada

MRQ

Printing 1, 2024

*This is for my pal Jackson Diehl, a Yalie, who has been my friend and colleague since we worked together in the* Washington Post's *Prince George's County bureau in 1978.*

*And it is for Buddy Teevens, who exemplified what the Ivy League is all about. I never got to see him coach a game in 2023, but he inspired me throughout the project.*

# CONTENTS

# THE ANCIENT EIGHT

# Introduction

IT ALL BEGAN WITH THE subway—specifically the IRT's number 1 train, which ran the length of Manhattan, from the battery to the northern tip of the island: last stop, 242nd Street.

By the time I was ten, I pretty much had the subway system down—especially the routes that ran to sports venues: the IRT took me downtown to Penn Station and Madison Square Garden, and the IND's D train landed at Yankee Stadium after I made the free transfer from IRT to IND at 59th Street. The number 7 train launched at Grand Central Station and became elevated after going under the East River from Manhattan to Queens and stopped, eventually, at Shea Stadium/Willets Point. At one point in my life I could name all twenty-one stops on the line. Shea Stadium was the twentieth.

And then there was the aforementioned number 1 train, which stopped at 215th Street, three blocks short of what was then Baker Field. If you want to watch the Columbia Lions play football today, you can get off at the same subway stop. The difference is you are now on your way to Robert K. Kraft Field at Lawrence A. Wien Stadium at the Baker Field Athletic Complex.

To me, it will always be Baker Field. Back then, it cost $4 to buy a ticket and there were always plenty of good seats available. Columbia had the occasional good player—quarterback Marty Domres, who played for nine seasons—one in the AFL and then eight in the NFL after the AFL and NFL merged in 1970—was one example. George Starke, who became known with the Washington Redskins as the leader of "The Hogs," was another. He was a good enough athlete to also play center on the basketball team.

During Domres's three seasons as a starter—when I was first riding the number 1 train to Baker Field—Columbia was 6–21, finishing 2–7 each season. Even so, Domres was the ninth pick in the 1969 AFL/NFL draft, going to the San Diego Chargers. He backed John Hadl up for three seasons, before being traded to the Baltimore Colts prior to the 1972 season.

When the Colts decided to bench thirty-nine-year-old Johnny Unitas six games into that season, it was Domres who started in his place.

That was about as close to football glory as Columbia got during those years. In 1961, Columbia went 6–3 overall and 6–1 in the Ivy League to tie for first place. To this day, that is Columbia's only conference title.

Despite Columbia's many losses, I enjoyed going to Baker Field. Not only could I always get good seats, but you could go down on the field after the game and mingle with the players. Once, I asked a visiting team captain if I could have the game ball he was carrying and he looked at me like I was from another planet.

"The game ball?" He said. "The game ball? Are you kidding?"

I figured it was worth a try.

Even after I went to college, I continued to follow Columbia and the Ivy League. In those days, the *New York Times* covered the Ivy

League as a beat, so I was able to read often about Columbia's forty-four-game losing streak—which began in 1983 and ended in 1988, three coaches later.

The *Washington Post*, where I began working after graduating from college in 1977, didn't cover the Ivy League very much, but I often found excuses to write about players and teams in both football and basketball. In 2017, after Al Bagnoli had miraculously turned Columbia football around, I wrote a piece about Columbia's 6–0 start. A defensive back named Landon Baty, who had been on teams that went 2–8 and 3–7 as a freshman and sophomore, told me a story about what a thrill it was when the counterman at Milano's Market on 113th Street gave him a complimentary chicken and turkey sandwich after the Lions had stunned Princeton.

I loved doing stories like that.

Which is why I wanted to write this book. I knew the players at all eight schools would have stories to tell. I also knew that one didn't have to be a first-round NFL draft pick to be someone who readers would want to know about. I'd learned that firsthand twenty-four years ago when I wrote a book titled *The Last Amateurs*, about basketball in the Patriot League.

My two closest advisers at the time—Esther Newberg, my agent, and Bob Woodward, yes, *the* Bob Woodward—both pleaded with me to not write that book. "Just write a nice, long magazine piece," Woodward counseled.

I almost always listen to Woodward—because he's about one hundred times smarter than I am—but my gut told me this was a book I wanted to do. Fortunately, Michael Pietsch, my editor at Little, Brown at the time, was willing to let me follow my gut. The book became a *New York Times* bestseller because there *were* so many stories to tell.

Which is what brought me to the Ivy League. In 2017, I did a book on playing quarterback in the NFL. One of the quarterbacks I focused on was Ryan Fitzpatrick, who had been a star at Harvard, graduating in 2005 with a degree in economics. Regardless of where he'd gone to college, Fitzpatrick was a remarkable story, having already spent twelve seasons in the NFL after being the 250th pick (out of 258) in the 2005 draft.

I was right. Fitzpatrick was smart (surprise), funny, and self-deprecating. The first time we met was at a sandwich shop in New Jersey (he had been with the Jets the previous season) that had no tables, just a counter.

Fitzpatrick was clearly comfortable in the blue-collar atmosphere. Harvard grad, wealthy NFL quarterback, comfortable anywhere.

That experience reminded me how much I had enjoyed talking to Ivy League athletes through the years. Which is why, after I finished a book on race in sports that I *needed* to write to save my soul, and a book on David Feherty, which was a joy to write, I thought again about the Ivy League.

To begin, the idea of writing about a conference that would *never* change was appealing. There was—and is—no chance that "The Ancient Eight" will ever become "The Ancient Ten" or "The Ancient Twelve."

The Big Ten, which loves to talk about its grand traditions, could now be called the Big 18. Once, its eastern-most school was Ohio State and Iowa was as far west as the league went. Now, Rutgers and Maryland are part of the league, and so are Washington (state!), UCLA, USC, and Oregon. The Big 12 now has sixteen teams, proof, if nothing else, that those running those conferences can't count very well. The Atlantic Coast Conference is now the home of Stanford and Cal-Berkeley—last seen located on the *Pacific* coast—and, wait for it, SMU. The Pac-12? Gone. Ten of the twelve teams have fled for bigger TV bucks.

Heck, even the Patriot League, which had seven teams when I wrote *The Last Amateurs*, now has ten teams. Seriously.

The Ivy League schools have played one another dating to the nineteenth century. Princeton played Rutgers in the first college football game *ever* in 1869. Yale celebrated its 150th year of football in 2023; Harvard its 149th. John Heisman—he of the Heisman Trophy—played for both Penn and Brown. Harvard claimed *eight* national championships, the *last* of them in 1919. When I first walked into Harvard Stadium (built in 1895), I asked Coach Tim Murphy what he remembered about that 1919 title. For the record, Tim and I are the same age.

More recently, Yale and Harvard played in arguably the most dramatic college football game ever, the 1968 game in which Harvard scored sixteen points in the last forty-two seconds to forge a 29–29 tie. There was no overtime in college football before 1996, which led to the famous Harvard Crimson headline: "Harvard beats Yale, 29–29."

Calvin Hill, later an NFL All-Pro running back in Dallas, played in that game for Yale as did quarterback Brian Dowling—immortalized by the great cartoonist Garry Trudeau, who just happened to be at Yale during those years, as "B.D." in his long-running *Doonesbury* comic strip. Trudeau actually created "B.D." while both he and Dowling were undergraduates in a strip called *Bull Tales*. That strip later became *Doonesbury*.

The Ivy League wasn't formally created until 1956, and the league presidents eventually got together to create rules and restrictions that guaranteed the one-time national powers would no longer be national powers. Now, Ivy League teams are often ranked in the

Football Championship Subdivision (FCS) rankings but, unlike in other sports, Ivy League champions don't get to participate in postseason play.

"It makes no sense," Yale coach Tony Reno said—echoing all the coaches and players in the league. "We only play ten games to start with. Why not let the kids who win the league championship get a chance to show people how good they are?"

This is yet another example of administrators mouthing clichés about "doing what's best for the 'student-athletes,'" then doing nothing to help the "student-athletes." Yup, even in the Ivy League, hypocrisy lives.

The two coaches who urged me to write this book were Tim Murphy and Buddy Teevens, the longtime coaches at Harvard and Dartmouth, both of whom I'd gotten to know fairly well. Murphy had come to Harvard in 1993 and was the school and the league's all-time winningest coach.

Teevens had been an All-Ivy League quarterback at Dartmouth in the 1970s and had also played on the hockey team when it went to the Frozen Four in 1978 (proof that in sports other than football, Ivy League postseason play is possible, perhaps even exciting).

The two men had been born eight days apart in 1956—Teevens on October 1, Murphy on October 9. Teevens was born in Pembroke, Massachusetts; Murphy in the neighboring town of Kingston. Each was about 35 miles from Boston.

They met at the age of twelve on a Little League baseball field when Murphy ran Teevens over trying to score. To this day he insists he was safe. Teevens—and the umpire—thought he was out.

They went to high school together and were football teammates and best friends. "I probably ate dinner at Buddy's house more often than at my house," Murphy likes to say.

Teevens went to Dartmouth while Murphy went to Springfield College—a late recruit.

"The thought that I would play college football never really crossed my mind until my senior year," Murphy said. "To be honest, I was thinking I would enlist in the marines."

He played linebacker at Springfield and then, at Teevens's urging, decided to give coaching a try after graduating. When Teevens became the coach at the University of Maine, he hired his pal as his offensive coordinator. The two men had worked together as assistant coaches at Boston University.

When Teevens was hired to be the head coach at his alma mater, he recommended that Murphy succeed him at Maine. Two years later, Murphy was hired at the University of Cincinnati. Teevens left Dartmouth in 1991 to coach at Tulane and later coached at Stanford after working for three years as an assistant under Steve Spurrier at Florida. With Dartmouth's program spiraling, he was brought back to the school in 2005. Murphy, after five seasons at Cincinnati, was hired at Harvard and never left.

The two men had remained best friends. Teevens was godfather to Murphy's first daughter; Murphy was godfather to Teevens's first daughter.

"He was my best friend for almost fifty-five years," Murphy said. "We'd even talked about going out together when it was time. Of course we never dreamed it would end this way."

Teevens, an inveterate bike rider, was hit by an F-150 truck on highway A1A in Florida on March 16, 2023. He lived a little more than six months with horrific injuries—he lost his right leg and was paralyzed from the shoulders down—before dying on September 26.

His longtime assistant coach Sammy McCorkle had been named acting coach after the accident and his pregame talk four days after

Teevens's death was as chilling as anything I've ever been privileged to hear in a locker room—and I've heard a lot of pregame talks in the last forty years.

I ended up interviewing about eighty players and all the Ivy League coaches to research this book. It would take a book twice as long as this one to properly tell all their stories. I can honestly say I enjoyed every interview I conducted. The players were everything you would want and expect Ivy League athletes to be. Driving up and down I-95 for four months was no picnic, but it was well worth it.

This isn't so much the story of one Ivy League football season—although that's certainly an important element—as it is the story of the remarkable young men who play Ivy League football and the older men who coach them.

Away from the football field, the school year among The Ancient Eight was, to say the least, tumultuous. Harvard president Claudine Gay and Penn president Liz Magill were forced to resign after testifying before Congress on December 5—seventeen days after the football season ended—on, among other topics, the Hamas-Israeli war.

When neither condemned the initial Hamas attack on October 7, calls for their resignation abounded. Four days later, after a little more than a year on the job, Magill resigned. Twenty-four days later, after only six months in her post, Gay, Harvard's first Black president, also resigned.

Then, in the spring, many campuses—most notably Columbia's—were engulfed in student protests on campus, almost all of them pro-Palestine, leaving Columbia president Minouche Shafik—the school's first woman president who had testified before Congress in April in favor of Israel—hanging on to her job for dear life.

The spring news stories were a place far away from the relative tranquility of fall football games.

My season was probably best summed up by the scene in the Harvard locker room after the Crimson lost 23–18 to Yale on the last day of the season. Even with the loss, Harvard tied for the Ivy League title—obviously, cold comfort when they could have won it outright. So there were plenty of tears in that locker room, but they weren't really all for the loss.

For most of the seniors, those tears were about the end of football: most would be going to graduate school or into the real world after graduation in May or, in some cases, in December. For the underclassmen, the tears were about the end of the 2023 Harvard football team. The seniors would be leaving and the underclassmen would all have to step into new roles beginning in the spring.

Tim Murphy hugged every player in the room. In the back of his mind, he knew this was likely to be his last game as Harvard's coach. He wasn't certain yet, but it was definitely something he'd been thinking about. That made the hugs more poignant. In a sense, he too was a senior. He understood exactly how his seniors felt in that moment. That's why his eyes were misty as he said farewell to all his players and to his coaches.

"When you've put everything you have into something for four years and you know it isn't going to be there anymore, you mourn for it," senior offensive tackle Jacob Rizy said. "You really don't want to take those pads off for the last time."

Most football players feel that way, but in the Ivy League it is more acute. They arrive knowing they will play no more than forty games in four years. There's no postseason to play for; only the Ivy League title and as many wins as possible. A handful will be graduate transfers, to a variety of programs, minor and major; a smaller handful will get a shot at the NFL.

Most know their last game as a senior is, in fact, their last game. They walk away with victories and defeats to remember.

"But no regrets," said Harvard offensive tackle Logan Bednar. "As long as we all know we've given absolutely everything we have to give, there are no regrets. We did that this past season. So, no regrets."

I saw both cheers and tears in Ivy League locker rooms last fall. But no regrets at all.

# Chapter One

**MARCH 17, 2023**

Sammy McCorkle had gotten to Boston's Logan Airport for his flight to Durham, North Carolina, early enough that he didn't have to rush to get to his gate. He'd flown out of Logan enough times to know you always leave extra time to deal with parking and security.

He was on his way to watch his daughter Madison (Maddy), a junior at Duke, play lacrosse against Syracuse. It wasn't that often that McCorkle, the defensive coordinator at Dartmouth, had time to take a day off and go see Maddy play. Now, with the start of spring practice a couple of weeks away, he had a window that allowed him to fly to Durham on Friday, watch the game on Saturday, and then take his daughter to dinner.

Normally, the idea of seeing his daughter play would put him in a buoyant mood, but, as much as he was looking forward to the trip, his mood was melancholy as he waited for his flight. The previous day he had learned that Josh Balara, who had been a starting offensive lineman for Dartmouth, had died after a protracted battle with cancer.

Balara's death wasn't a huge surprise. He had been forced to drop out of school during the fall semester and when he had visited for a game, everyone could see how sick he looked.

"It wasn't a shock," McCorkle said. "But it *was* a shock. I mean, he was twenty-one years old."

McCorkle was trying to relax before his flight when his phone rang. He was surprised to see that it was athletic director Mike Harrity, who had been on the job for less than a year. McCorkle couldn't think of a reason why Harrity would be calling him. He suspected it wasn't to wish Maddy good luck the next afternoon.

Harrity made no attempt at small talk. He let McCorkle know that associate athletic director Don Whitmore was on the phone too and suggested he find a quiet place to talk. McCorkle walked to a quiet spot away from where other passengers were sitting.

The news wasn't bad—it was worse than bad.

"Buddy was in an accident last night," Harrity said. "A very serious one."

He then filled McCorkle in on what he knew: Teevens and his wife Kirsten had been vacationing during spring break at their home south of Jacksonville. They had ridden their bicycles to a nearby restaurant for dinner.

En route home, Teevens had been crossing highway A1A when he was slammed into by a Ford F-150 truck. The driver hadn't been speeding—she was going about 40 miles per hour according to the police report—but couldn't stop before slamming into Teevens.

The injuries were horrific. His spine had been crushed and one of his legs had to be amputated right away. Whether he would ever coach again was in serious doubt. An email was being sent to all of

Dartmouth's players asking them to make themselves available for an emergency Zoom meeting at seven o'clock the next night. Because of spring break, very few of them were on campus.

"I still went to the game," McCorkle said. "There was really nothing I could do at that point. But the phone calls never stopped during the game."

After Duke had lost to second-ranked Syracuse, 16–10, Maddy greeted her father by asking, "What's wrong?"

"She knew I never talked on the phone when she was playing, so something had to be going on."

McCorkle had very few details but he knew enough to say, "Something terrible has happened."

He wasn't exaggerating.

On that same morning, Tim Murphy and his wife, Martha, were en route to the airport north of Naples to fly home to Boston after their spring vacation. The phone rang. It was Lindsay Teevens, Buddy and Kirsten's oldest child and Tim Murphy's goddaughter. She told the Murphys that her father had been in a terrible accident on his bicycle the night before and was at the Mayo Clinic in Jacksonville.

"We just kept driving," Murphy said. "Never went to the airport. It took about four hours to get to the hospital. By the time we got there, the doctors had already amputated Buddy's leg and he was about to go into surgery again."

Murphy was allowed to briefly see his lifelong friend. "He couldn't talk, but he could communicate by blinking his eyes," Murphy said. "Looking back, it's amazing that he survived the accident at all. The doctor told me he had to go right back in for more surgery. I was in complete shock."

Like a lot of men and women of his generation, Buddy Teevens didn't wear a helmet when on his bike. He had ridden cross-country several years earlier as part of a charity fundraiser—all without a helmet. Whether a helmet would have made any difference that evening is impossible to say, but given the battering his entire body took, it is unlikely.

Most of Dartmouth's players were spread out around the country on spring break when they got a message from director of football operations Dino Cauteruccio telling them there would be an emergency Zoom meeting for the entire team Saturday night at seven o'clock. McCorkle was in his hotel room in Durham when the meeting took place.

Harrity opened the meeting by talking briefly about Balara, knowing the players were keenly aware of his death. Then he told them that he had another piece of bad news he needed to relate to them.

"I think it hit us all like a ton of bricks," quarterback Nick Howard said. "It felt like it couldn't be true. Even though he didn't give us a lot of detail, we knew it had to be very serious for them to call a special Zoom meeting. We knew the meeting wasn't about Josh, because we all knew already that he had passed away. So, we were expecting something bad, but not like that."

Harrity told the players that McCorkle would be the acting coach. That made sense. He had come to Dartmouth in 2005 when Teevens had returned for his second stint as head coach. He was Teevens's top assistant and the plan had been for him to move up and take over the program when Teevens retired.

"That was the plan," McCorkle said. "But not this way and not this soon."

McCorkle was fifty. He had gone to Florida as a walk-on and had been a team captain on Steve Spurrier's 1996 national championship team. After one year as a high school coach, he'd returned to Florida as a graduate assistant coach. That was where he met Teevens, who had gone to work for Spurrier after being fired as the head coach at Tulane.

When Teevens returned to Dartmouth in 2005 following a stint at Stanford, he offered McCorkle a job coaching his defensive backs and special teams. They had been together ever since.

"When he was named interim coach the next week, he never said we're moving on," Howard said. "He said we're moving forward, which was exactly what Coach T would have said. That's exactly what we did, we moved forward. We knew Coach T wouldn't have wanted it any other way and Coach Mac wasn't going to have it any other way either."

Ten days after the accident, Dartmouth began spring practice. Even then, very few people at Dartmouth knew exactly how seriously he had been hurt. Tim Murphy did know how serious the injuries to his friend had been.

"I don't see any way he can ever coach again," he said, one morning sitting in his office. "But if anyone is strong enough to come back from something like this, it's Buddy. I'm just not sure that anybody is that strong."

Teevens was moved first from the Mayo Clinic in Jacksonville to a hospital in Atlanta that specialized in dealing with severe spinal injuries and then, eventually, to a similar hospital in Boston, if only to make things easier for his family—Boston being two hours away from Hanover, New Hampshire, where Dartmouth is located.

The Dartmouth football team remained in limbo. McCorkle and the rest of the staff, most of whom had been at Dartmouth working for Teevens for years, had no idea what would happen if Teevens could not return.

Deep down, the players knew that Coach T wasn't coming back.

"It was one of those things where the lack of information was a pretty clear hint," said Grayson O'Bara, a wide receiver who had almost died in an ATV accident (he was a passenger) while in high school. "If it had been less serious, they probably would have given us more details. As it was, it was pretty frustrating."

All of that left the entire team in a state of uncertainty, including the coaches. McCorkle stayed in his office, more as a symbolic gesture than anything else. In fact, even after Teevens's death, he remained in his small assistant coach's office.

"I wouldn't feel right in there," he said just before the season started. "That's Buddy's office. I'm here in this office because he brought me here eighteen years ago and I'm just fine with that."

The Ivy League doesn't get very much media coverage except when tragedy strikes or when Yale plays Harvard. Most who cover the league regularly are bloggers or those who work for student newspapers. That's why the Ivy League's preseason poll consisted of only sixteen voters. If there had been eighty voters, the results probably would have been the same.

Yale, the defending champion, returned many key players, most notably quarterback Nolan Grooms, who had been the Ivy League Offensive Player of the Year, as a junior. Princeton, which had finished tied for second (and also returned its starting quarterback), was picked second; Penn was picked third; Harvard fourth; Columbia fifth; Dartmouth sixth; Cornell seventh; and Brown eighth.

The Eli got thirteen of the sixteen first-place votes. Princeton got one, Harvard got one, and Columbia got one.

The bottom five teams in the poll all took being picked that low personally.

"It was a chip-on-the-shoulder type of thing," Tim Murphy said. "We were *never* picked below third, usually first or second. We'd had a down year for us in 2022 [6–4, 4–3 in conference play], but we knew we were going to be better than that. It gave us a little bit of a rallying cry going into the season."

The same was true for every team picked in the second division. "We're thinking about winning the conference—as in finishing first," said Brown's star wide receiver, Wes Rockett. "We were close in every game last season. This season we want to take the next step and finish those close games."

In Dartmouth's locker room, you often heard the word "sixth!" As in, "They picked us sixth! No way!"

All eight teams honestly believed they had a chance to win a championship. "You know every game is going to be close, you just take it for granted," said Princeton quarterback Blake Stenstrom. "Last year we were one play—ONE play—from tying for the conference title. That's the way we assume it will be this year—every week. One play in the fourth quarter."

The league had ended 2022 with as experienced a group of head coaches as anywhere in the country. Murphy led the way having coached twenty-eight years at Harvard; his pal Teevens was next with twenty-two seasons in two stints at Dartmouth; Al Bagnoli had been in the league for thirty years—twenty-three at Penn and seven at Columbia; Princeton's Bob Surace had been the head coach for twelve seasons; Tony Reno had been at Yale for ten years; Dave Archer had been Cornell's coach for nine years; Ray Priore had succeeded Bagnoli and had led Penn for seven years and had been at the school since 1987. The "rookie" in the group was Brown's James Perry, who had coached three years.

Four of the eight coaches were at their alma maters: Teevens, Surace, Archer, and Perry.

In a different sense, you could have called *them* "The Ancient Eight."

They all knew one another and some (notably Teevens and Murphy) were friends. The most successful ones had had opportunities to leave for bigger, better-paying jobs. The only one who had left at any point was Teevens, who had been the coach at Tulane and Stanford in the 1990s before returning to Dartmouth for good in 2005.

By the start of the 2023 season, there were two new head coaches, although neither had been named head coach. Sammy McCorkle had been an assistant at Dartmouth under Teevens since 2005. He was named acting coach and then interim coach after Teevens's bicycle accident.

Mark Fabish had been recruited by Al Bagnoli to play at Penn and had been an assistant coach under him there after graduating. He had moved with Bagnoli to Columbia in 2015 and was named head coach on August 4, 2023, after Bagnoli decided to retire following a heart procedure in the spring.

"I just don't feel like I have the energy to go through ten- to twelve-hour days for fourteen weeks (preseason practice and the season) without a day off with the enthusiasm I need to do the job right," he said at the time. "I'm seventy. I think it's time."

Neither Fabish nor McCorkle had ever been a head coach, but they brought plenty of experience at their schools to their new jobs. McCorkle was fifty, Fabish forty-nine. Each walked into a difficult situation: McCorkle was taking over in the wake of a tragedy; Fabish had exactly six weeks from the day he was named until opening day. Plus, both were carrying "interim" tags, meaning neither they nor their staffs nor their players knew what the future held.

"It's certainly not easy," Fabish said, standing on the field before Columbia's opening game at Lafayette, "but I have to look at it as an opportunity. It's up to me to take advantage of the opportunity. It's up to all of us."

There was one other coach whose future was in doubt—and he knew it. Dave Archer was about as purely a Cornell man as anyone alive. He had grown up in nearby Endicott, New York, and had turned down a chance to play for Harvard to go to Cornell. He was a three-year starter on the offensive line and captain of the team in 2005—a year in which the Big Red went 6–4, a rare winning record.

He had taught and coached at Fairleigh Dickinson for one year, before Coach Jim Knowles brought him back in 2007 as an assistant. Six seasons later, he'd been named the head coach at the age of thirty, making him the youngest head coach in the country at the time.

There was no doubting that Archer had put heart and soul into turning Cornell around. Like Columbia, the Big Red had always struggled in Ivy League play. It had shared the Ivy League title on three occasions: 1971 (when Ed Marinaro, eventual NFL player and television actor, was the team's star), 1988, and 1991. It's last winning season had been 2005—Archer's senior year.

Now though, with quarterback Jameson Wang—who Archer thought had the potential to be the Ivy League Player of the Year—and with a number of key players returning from a team that had finished 5–5, Archer's first nonlosing record, there was reason to believe the Big Red could compete with anyone in the league.

Wins over Dartmouth and Brown the year before and close losses to Harvard and Penn had given everybody hope.

"We were close last year," Wang said. "Closer than people outside the program really know. This year though we don't want to be close, we want to take the next step and that means competing for an Ivy League title."

All eight teams arrived at opening day, two weeks after most college teams had started their twelve-game seasons, believing this could be—would be—their year.

"I can't wait to get started," Murphy said. "And I've been a head coach for thirty-eight years."

Or, as Columbia's Mason Tomlin (son of Steelers coach Mike) said after making the tackle on the opening kickoff against Lafayette, "Playing this game never gets old."

# Chapter Two

THE 2023 IVY LEAGUE FOOTBALL season officially/unofficially began at 6:00 p.m. on March 24 when the University of Pennsylvania held its first practice of the spring.

The Ivy League is part of the Football Championship Subdivision (FCS), which is the second highest level of college football—higher than Division 2 and Division 3 and below the Football Bowl Subdivision (FBS), which is where the superrich teams like Alabama, Georgia, Michigan, and Notre Dame play.

While the FBS teams are allowed fifteen spring practice days, the Ivy League allows only twelve. Until 1992, spring practice in the Ivy League consisted of *one* day, which was known as "media day," and had very little to do with any actual practice.

"Basically it was a day to get together, talk to the media, and then have a cookout," said Princeton coach Bob Surace, who played center at Princeton from 1986 to 1989 and became the Tigers' coach in 2010. "There really wasn't much point in trying to do anything else when you only had one day."

Now, the twelve days of spring are carefully mapped out because the coaches must work around the players' academic schedules. That's why they start on different days—and end on different days. In 2023, Penn was the first team to start. For the fun of it—nothing more—the first practice, which was on a Friday, was dubbed "Friday Night Lights" by coach Ray Priore, an homage to the famous book about high school football and to the fact that six conference games during the season were to be televised by ESPNU on Fridays, giving the players a chance to play on national television.

Harvard-Yale, the biggest game of the season in the league, regardless of standings, is always televised by one of ESPN's channels on the Saturday before Thanksgiving—the last weekend of the ten-game Ivy League season.

The Ivy League only played nine games each season—seven conference games and two nonconference games—until 1977 when a tenth nonconference game was added. All ten games are played over a stretch of ten straight weeks. Power schools generally have at least two bye weeks to rest and heal injuries. In fact, in 2023 Navy played its first game on August 26, three weeks before the Ivies opened play, and its final game (against Army) on December 9, three weeks after the Ivy League finales.

"It goes fast, but it's also exhausting," Cornell quarterback Jameson Wang said. "One minute you're preparing for game one, the next you're shaking hands after the last game of the season. That's usually when you notice that your whole body aches."

There's a saying in football—at every level—that players must understand the difference between being hurt and being injured. If you're hurt, you keep playing. Only if you have a real injury do you stop playing. Occasionally you even keep playing injured.

In the penultimate game of the 2023 season, Penn defensive end Joey Slackman tore a tendon in his arm late in the Quakers' game against Harvard. The team doctor examined the arm and told Slackman he was going to need surgery. His senior season was over.

A few minutes later, the game went into overtime. Slackman told the doctor he was going back into the game. "It was a complete tear," he said. "I couldn't tear it any more."

Slackman not only returned, but he made a goal line tackle to stretch the game into a third overtime. Harvard won 25–23 on a two-point play dubbed "Crimson Special," a copy of the Philadelphia Eagles' famous "Philly Special" (a play involving a snap to the running back, rather than to the quarterback, a pitch to the tight end, then a pass to the quarterback) that had helped the Eagles win Super Bowl LII against the New England Patriots.

"It was heartbreaking," Slackman said. "But I went out the way I wanted to—playing with something to play for—not standing on the sideline feeling helpless."

Slackman was a remarkable story, having come to Penn as a wrestler who walked on to the football team and was a team captain by his senior year. He wasn't that unusual among Ivy League players in that he improved every year after not being a starter for his first year or two.

Yale had won the Ivy League title in 2022 with a record of 6–1 in conference play, meaning it finished one game ahead of Princeton and Penn. The biggest surprise of that season was the Dartmouth Big Green, which had finished 9–1 in 2018, 2019, and 2021—there was no Ivy League football season due to COVID in 2020—and perennially challenged for first place.

But in 2022, the Big Green had finished 2–5 in conference play and 3–7 overall. It was the second time since 2010 that Dartmouth had finished below .500 overall and just the second time it had finished lower than third in the conference.

"I think all of us, players and coaches, began to take things a little bit for granted," said Sammy McCorkle early in spring practice. "Buddy put a major emphasis on that once our season was over. Once, there was a margin for error in some games in the Ivy League, but that's not true anymore. No game is a walkover. All you have to do is look at the standings every year to know that's true."

The biggest reason for that change was Columbia, which had been the league doormat forever. The league had been officially formed in 1956 and Columbia had won the football championship in 1961 for the first and only time.

Between that first official season and 2014, Columbia had *four* winning seasons and won more than six games twice. During one torturous stretch in the 1980s, the Lions lost forty-four games in a row—a record for futility that still stands. There were three winless seasons and a 1–9 season under three different coaches during that stretch.

Ray Tellier took over in 1989 and actually managed two winning seasons, including going 8–2 in 1996. He lasted twelve seasons in all, going 1–9 in 2002—far more normal for Columbia than the remarkable 8–2. The next three coaches—Bob Shoop, Norries Wilson, and Pete Mangurian—went a combined 27–93, with the 2005 team under Wilson producing a 5–5 record, the only nonlosing season in twelve years. The Lions were 0–10 during Mangurian's last two seasons.

All of which led, strangely enough, to Eldo Bagnoli, better known as Al, changing the culture at Columbia and for the entire league.

"Al made Columbia consistently competitive," Tim Murphy said. "Once, if you lost to Columbia, you thought something was seriously wrong. That stopped being the case once Al got there."

Bagnoli, who was born in Italy before his parents immigrated to Connecticut when he was four years old, had been an undersized defensive back at Central Connecticut State who knew that coaching was what he wanted to do when he graduated in 1975. He became a graduate assistant at the University of Albany and was soon promoted to defensive coordinator.

In 1978, he was hired as the defensive coordinator at Division 3 Union College in Schenectady, New York—a few miles down the road from Albany. Four years later, at the age of twenty-nine, he was hired as Union's head coach. He quickly turned Union into a D-3 power, going 86–19 in ten seasons, including six appearances in the D-3 tournament, twice reaching the championship game.

When Penn fired Coach Gary Steele in 1991 after he'd had three losing seasons, it offered Bagnoli the job. For the next twenty-one years, Penn was the Ivy League's most successful program. The Quakers won nine outright conference titles, had three undefeated seasons, and did not have a losing season during that stretch. In 1997, one of their players, Mitch Marrow, dropped several classes, making him ineligible. Penn forfeited five wins, which technically turned its record to 1–9.

In 2013 and 2014, the Quakers had their first real losing seasons under Bagnoli, going 4–6 and 2–8. At the end of the 2014 season, Bagnoli, who was sixty-one at the time, announced he was retiring to become an administrator in the Penn athletic department. Even with the two losing seasons, Bagnoli's record at Penn was 148–80.

His retirement lasted ninety-two days. Columbia was—again—searching for a coach. Pete Mangurian had gone 3–27 in three seasons and the Lions had lost twenty-one games in a row. Their last winning season had been in 1996.

Athletic director Peter Pilling, who had been on the job for less than a month, decided to take a long-shot chance, looking for a coach who knew how to win in the Ivy League. That led to a phone call to Bagnoli to ask if he really was ready to retire as a coach.

Two weeks later, Bagnoli was introduced as Columbia's new coach, which got the attention of everyone in the Ivy League, including his successor at Penn, Ray Priore.

"I'd been his assistant for twenty-three years," Priore said. "I *knew* he would change things at Columbia."

Columbia extended its latest losing streak by opening the 2015 season with three straight losses, meaning it had lost twenty-four straight games. In week four, it beat Wagner 24–6, giving the seniors their first victory since they had been freshmen.

Pilling kept his promise to improve facilities at the Baker Field Athletic Complex—including building the "Baker Bubble," which went up over the soccer field as soon as the fall season was complete, giving Columbia an indoor practice facility for the winter months. The school even got permission to use the West Side Highway for its buses to take players from the campus at 116th and Broadway to the Baker complex at 218th and Broadway for practice each day.

The West Side Highway is generally closed to buses, and the difference between traveling on the highway versus weaving through traffic lights going uptown and downtown on Broadway was usually twenty minutes each way.

"Makes a huge difference," Bagnoli said. "Especially in recruiting."

The players are told, especially by outside recruiters, about the daily trip. Most say that they not only get used to it but they also look forward to it.

"You get on the bus and you can just click your mind off after classes and before football," said senior defensive back Mason Tomlin.

The only other school in the league where the team practices off-campus is Yale. The practice facility is the Yale Bowl, which is about a ten-minute bus trip from campus, depending on the city traffic the bus must weave through.

After two more losing seasons, raising the number of consecutive nonwinning seasons to twenty (the Lions had gone 5–5 in 2006), Bagnoli's recruiting and coaching began to kick in.

In week three of the 2017 season, the Lions beat Princeton for the first time since 1996. A week later they beat Penn—also for the first time in twenty years. The wins made them 4–0.

Landon Baty, who was a senior defensive back on that team, vividly remembers walking to Milano's, a deli on 113th Street, for his daily lunch—a chicken and turkey cutlets sandwich—on the Monday after the Princeton game.

"I was wearing a Columbia football shirt," he said. "As the guy was cutting my sandwich, he was going on and on about the Princeton game and how much fun it was to watch our team play."

"It occurred to me that my first three seasons I would never be caught wearing a football shirt around campus. None of us would. We'd wear nonfootball gear, keep our heads down, and hope no one asked how the team was doing."

Columbia ended up 8–2 that season, losing only to Harvard and Yale. It went into the season's final Saturday with a chance to tie for the Ivy League title if it could beat Brown and Harvard could beat Yale. The Lions held up their end, beating Brown 24–6, but Yale beat Harvard, 24–3, to win the title with a 6–1 league record, a game better than Columbia.

That season marked the end of Columbia's days as the conference doormat and perennial walkover game.

"It wasn't just that they began to win games," Princeton coach Bob Surace said. "It was that when you played them, win or lose, you knew they were going to be a tough out. They were tough and they were physical and you knew that winning was a big deal, just like beating anyone else in the league was a big deal."

Columbia had only one losing season from 2017 through 2022. It went 30–20 during those years, which was remarkable given that the ten men who had coached the Lions dating to 1956 had all left the school with losing records.

Bagnoli was keenly aware of what Columbia had been prior to his arrival. At Penn, he had gone 21–2 against Columbia. "We lost one game in overtime and the other one when Marcellus Wiley [who played in the NFL for ten years] blocked an extra point to keep the game from going into overtime," he said. "I remembered both those games vividly."

Bagnoli liked to joke that explaining the difference between coaching at Penn and coaching at Columbia was easy. "At Penn if we lost two in a row, I'd hear murmurs that maybe it was time for the old coach to hang it up," he said. "At Columbia, when we won two in a row, they'd want to build a statue to me."

That may well happen in the near future.

Al Bagnoli was getting ready for his thirtieth season as an Ivy League head coach in March of 2023. "I felt fine," he said. "A little bit tired at times, but nothing you wouldn't expect just after your seventieth birthday."

His annual physical came up with a different reason for his fatigue: he had a blockage in one of his arteries, hardly uncommon for someone who had worked in a highly stressful job. His doctor suggested putting in a stent to open the blockage—a fairly simple procedure in this day and age. The procedure was successful and he was ready to go to work when spring ball started.

The Lions had gone 6–4 in 2022 and had most of their key players back on defense. The defense had become their calling card under Bagnoli and there was no reason to believe it would not again be the heart and soul of the team. Columbia would be picked fifth in the preseason conference poll.

"The thing is those polls mean very little," said Yale coach Tony Reno, whose team had won the league in 2022. "Almost every game you play is going to come down to one or two plays in the fourth quarter. We finished first last year. We could just as easily have been fourth. It's that way just about every year."

That may sound like coach-speak, but the 2022 season backed Reno up. On the final day of the season, Yale won at Harvard and then the players, families, and friends stood around on the field at Harvard Stadium to wait for the outcome of the Princeton-Penn game.

Penn drove the length of the field in the final minutes, scoring a touchdown with five seconds left on a 5-yard pass from Aidan Sayin to Trey Flowers for a 20–19 victory. The Princeton faithful were convinced that the play clock had run out before the snap but the officials didn't see it that way.

Penn's victory meant that Yale won the outright title with Princeton and Penn a game back and Harvard another game behind. If Princeton and Harvard had won on that Saturday, there would have been a three-way tie for first.

Bagnoli came out of spring practice feeling two things: that Columbia had a chance to be very good come the fall, and he wasn't sure if he had the energy needed to give the Lions their best chance for success.

"Ivy League football is a sprint," he said. "From mid-August (when preseason practice begins) until the Saturday before Thanksgiving, there are no days off. You play ten straight weeks—no byes; no time for players to get a break if they're sore or banged up. No time for coaches to recharge. I just didn't feel as if I could recharge the way I needed to recharge."

Bagnoli was thinking seriously about retiring as soon as spring practice ended. He'd gotten through it feeling fine, but spring ball in the Ivy League is twelve practices in five weeks—no back-to-back days. Once summer practice began on August 18, there would be no days off until the finale on November 18.

"I'd been through it before and I knew how exhausting it was," Bagnoli said. "I just didn't think I was ready to go through it again."

He waited to make a final decision for two reasons: he wanted to see if postspring/presummer down time would make him feel better and he wanted to be sure his staff would remain intact once he announced his decision. He wanted to be sure that Mark Fabish, who had played for him at Penn and then coached under him at both Penn and Columbia, would get the job.

And so he waited until August 4 to announce that he was stepping down. Fabish would be the interim head coach. That meant that what had been the most stable league in college football would start the season with two longtime assistants, Fabish and Dartmouth's Sammy McCorkle, in roles as interim head coaches.

The stability prior to 2023 was indicative of two things: The Ivy League tends to give coaches a longer leash than their FBS peers—Teevens had gone 0–10 in his fourth consecutive losing season in 2008 before turning Dartmouth around, and most coaches had dealt with losing seasons early before turning the corner. In addition, most coaches were happy coaching Ivy League players and had no desire to leave once they were established.

Most had a chance to leave for FBS jobs that would pay more money than the Ivy League. "What's the old saying, 'Why run away from happiness?'" Murphy said. "I love my life, I enjoy coming to work every day, I love coaching a team that's part of a league that's never going to be part of realignment. That's why I've never gone after some of the jobs I might have had."

His former assistant, Tony Reno, who had turned Yale around after arriving in 2012, felt pretty much the same way. "Coaching in the Ivy League is fun, especially nowadays," he said. "We still get to *coach*. We have a few kids with small NILs, but we aren't out raising money for them. We have transfers, but not very many either coming or going. When we recruit a kid, chances are we're going to have him for four years."

Teevens's accident and Bagnoli's retirement changed the mood in the league. Teevens's accident not only cast a pall over spring practice at Dartmouth but was felt all around the league.

"Buddy's impact on football goes beyond Dartmouth," said Perry, who had been the Ivy League Player of the Year at Brown in 1999. "The safety innovations that he pushed for are a lot more important than any of the games or championships he ever won."

It was Teevens who first suggested cutting back on hitting in practice when chronic traumatic encephalopathy (CTE) was first recognized as a serious issue for football players. Not only did he cut contact drills back at Dartmouth, but he also pushed for other schools to do the same. Many schools in the Ivy League and many around the country followed Teevens's example, especially after students and staff at Dartmouth's engineering school invented a robotic tackling dummy that was dubbed MVP—Mobile Virtual Player—that not only controlled contact but also showed players the proper technique for tackling. Today, MVP is used by numerous colleges and some NFL teams.

"I still remember the first time Buddy brought it up to me," said Cornell coach Dave Archer. "I had been thinking I needed to come up with a way to cut down on tackling in practice but I never thought, 'How do I do this to make the game better for everyone?' My thought was how to make the game better for my team. Buddy was always thinking about ways to make football better, not just to make Dartmouth football better."

Although Dartmouth was very discreet about the seriousness of Teevens's injuries, the league grapevine—especially among the coaches—made it clear that he was in very tough shape. The police description of the accident alone—an F-150 truck hitting someone on a bicycle in the middle of a highway—told people how serious the accident had been. Teevens was moved from the hospital in Jacksonville to a spinal specialty hospital in Atlanta and then to Boston.

McCorkle was named acting head coach right away and then interim coach, but with a new athletic director, neither he nor anyone on the staff knew what would come next. It was very much a veteran staff, with six of the assistants having been at Dartmouth for at least nine years and three others having been there at least six years.

"It's the kind of place where once you get here, you really don't want to leave," said wide receivers coach David Shula, a former NFL head coach and the son of Hall of Fame NFL coach Don Shula. "I think everyone on this staff would be able to find another job, but none of us want to do that. We all love it here."

And they all loved working for Teevens, who treated his staff more like partners than subordinates.

"If snow needed to be shoveled or plowed, Buddy would be the first one out there," McCorkle said. "If the rest of us went out to help, that was fine, but he never asked us to do anything he wouldn't do himself."

All of that left Dartmouth in a state of preseason uncertainty and anxiety. The coaches knew that Teevens wasn't coming back, even though they didn't discuss it much. And they had no idea what the school would do after the season if Teevens didn't return.

"It's difficult for everyone," senior quarterback Nick Howard said. "We were all recruited by Coach T; he's a big part of the reason we came to Dartmouth. But one way or another, this doesn't change what happens to us after we graduate. The coaches own houses, have families who love it up here, and now they have no idea what comes next. I can't imagine how difficult that is for them."

And so, as the grind of preseason practice played out, two of the eight schools were very much in flux. But the other six were on firm ground, and the players at every single school were convinced they had the ability to finish at the top of the league.

They couldn't all be right.

# Chapter Three

THERE WASN'T ANY DOUBT THAT the preseasons at Dartmouth and Columbia were the most difficult of the eight Ivy League schools.

Dartmouth's players and coaches were dealing with both tragedy and uncertainty—the coaches had a better idea than the players how serious Buddy Teevens's injuries were but had no idea what their future would hold if Teevens—as seemed likely—didn't return.

Columbia was merely dealing with uncertainty. Dartmouth had spring practice to adapt to Sammy McCorkle in the role of head coach and the rest of the staff moving into new roles because of McCorkle's promotion, but Columbia had very little time to deal with its coaching change. Al Bagnoli didn't announce his retirement until August 4—two weeks prior to the start of preseason practice and six before the season opener against Lafayette on September 16.

"On August 3rd, I was still the offensive coordinator," Mark Fabish said. "On August 4th, I was the coach. Those are two very different jobs."

One thing McCorkle and Fabish had in common was the term *interim*. Neither had any idea when or if he would have the word removed from his title.

"There's no more insecure word in sports than *interim*," Fabish said. "It kind of hangs over you."

Emotionally, though, the coach having the most difficult time was Harvard's Tim Murphy. Teevens's best friend would turn sixty-seven in October and the word hanging over his head wasn't *interim*; it was *retirement*.

When Murphy would retire was strictly up to him. He had first come to Harvard in 1994 after turning around a struggling program at the University of Cincinnati. In twenty-eight seasons, he had gone 192–87 and had won nine Ivy League titles. Three of his teams had gone 10–0 and he was 19–9 against Yale. He was the winningest coach in Ivy League history and two of the league's head coaches—Tony Reno at Yale and James Perry at Brown—had worked as assistants under him.

As a group, Ivy League coaches get along quite well. They aren't any less competitive than coaches in other leagues, but there's a bond in coaching in a league that is different from all others: the academics, the need to figure out scholarship packages for players, the inability to compete in postseason, the ten-games-with-no-off-weeks schedule.

"Let's face it, at many, if not most, schools that play football, the sport is the school's front porch for most people," Yale coach Tony Reno said. "In the Ivy League, academics will always be the front porch. It doesn't mean football doesn't matter—it does, but academics will always be our calling card."

Many coaches have Ivy League backgrounds. Going into 2023, before Teevens's accident, four of the eight head coaches—Teevens,

Perry, Dave Archer, and Bob Surace—were coaching their alma maters. Ray Priore had been a Penn assistant for twenty years before becoming the head coach, and Al Bagnoli had coached at two different schools for a total of thirty years.

When McCorkle took over for Teevens in March of 2023, he had been an assistant under him since 2005, the year Teevens had returned to Dartmouth. Fabish had played and coached for Bagnoli at Penn before moving with him to Columbia.

The closest relationship in the league belonged to Murphy and Teevens, who had first met on a Little League baseball field at the age of twelve and had been best friends ever since.

"We had a collision at home plate," Murphy said. "I thought I was safe, Buddy thought I was out. Unfortunately, the umpire sided with him. We never really stopped arguing about it."

They were high school teammates before Teevens went to Dartmouth and Murphy went to Springfield College. Teevens's family had Dartmouth connections: his father had lettered in hockey and his younger brother and sister would follow him there as athletes. He was the Ivy League Player of the Year in 1978, quarterbacking the Big Green to the Ivy League title. He was also part of the school's hockey team that went to the 1979 Frozen Four.

Murphy had no such connections and, in fact, didn't think he was going to go to college at all. "The plan was to enlist in the marines when I finished high school," he said.

His plans changed when he began receiving interest as a linebacker from a number of schools, notably Springfield, in western Massachusetts. Figuring the marines would still be there, and that getting a college degree wasn't a bad idea, Murphy went to Springfield where he started at linebacker for four years and majored in business.

He started his coaching career as a graduate assistant at Brown and went to work at Maine in 1985—the head coach who hired him was Buddy Teevens. When Teevens was hired to coach at Dartmouth, he recommended Murphy to succeed him. Murphy went 13–8 at Maine, winning the Yankee Conference and reaching the NCAA FCS tournament (then called 1-AA) in his first season. That got the attention of Cincinnati, which had just gone 1–10 and was looking for a young coach to change the losing culture. In 1989, Murphy, who was thirty-two when the season started, became the youngest FBS coach in the country.

After going 1–9–1 in his first season and 1–10 in his second, Murphy gradually turned the Bearcats around, going 8–3 in 1993—his fifth season. That was a school record for victories. At the same time, Cincinnati started doing a much better job graduating players. Cincinnati had combined poor players with poor students before Murphy's arrival. He was able to turn both things around.

All of which got the attention of Harvard. Technically, a move from an FBS school like Cincinnati to an FCS school like Harvard was a step down in terms of football. But Murphy didn't see it that way. He'd grown up not far from Harvard, and his pal Teevens, who had been the coach at Dartmouth for five years, had told him about how enjoyable it was to coach Ivy League players.

"It just felt like a unique opportunity to me," he said. "Plus, when I met the members of the selection committee, I remember thinking, 'If these are the kind of people I'll be working for, this has to be a good job.'"

Murphy took a 50 percent pay cut to move from Cincinnati to Harvard and never regretted it.

Harvard had only had two coaches dating to 1957: John Yovicsin, from 1957 to 1970, and Joe Restic, who took over in 1970 and coached the team for twenty-three years. Murphy had no idea that he would coach Harvard for longer than both men.

Murphy had chances to return to 1-A but never seriously thought about leaving. After three losing seasons under Murphy, Harvard won the Ivy League title in 1997 with a 9–1 record. Beginning in 2001, the Crimson had sixteen straight winning seasons and won eight more Ivy League titles.

Often the team that beat Harvard for the championship was Dartmouth. Teevens had returned in 2005 after stints at Tulane and Stanford and, like Murphy at Harvard, had struggled in his first few seasons. In fact, the Big Green went 9–41 his first five seasons back—including going 0–10 in 2008. But Dartmouth stuck with him, in part because he was an alum but also because he had won Ivy League titles in his last two seasons during his first stint at the school.

"They knew he was going to be the right guy for their school," Murphy said. "That's something that will happen at an Ivy League school but not many other places."

Teevens and Dartmouth tied Harvard for the league title in 2015 and then tied with Yale for the title in 2019 and 2021. Between 2018 and 2021, the Big Green went 27–3 overall.

Teevens's accident and seeing up close what his friend looked like lying in his hospital bed the day after the accident shook Murphy. Teevens's friendship and the fact that playing Dartmouth would always make for an emotional and competitive afternoon were givens in his life. Their wives were best friends. Each man had asked the other to be godfather to his first child.

"I honestly can't remember a time when Buddy wasn't in my life," Murphy said. "Fifty-five years is a long time. My memory as a kid is that I ate dinner at his house more than at my own. Of course on a lot of the nights that I did eat at home, Buddy was at our house for dinner."

They had coached against one another for seventeen seasons—the 2020 pandemic year being the only exception—and had talked about perhaps retiring together when the time came. "It was definitely something we talked about," Murphy said. "But we never talked about it happening *this* way."

After Teevens had been moved to Boston—in part for the specialized spinal treatment he needed and in part to make it easier for his family to make the two-hour trip from Hanover to see him—Murphy and his wife, Martha, visited him regularly. By then Teevens could talk, but he was still paralyzed from the chest down and still clearly in a good deal of pain.

On the morning of September 12—four days before Harvard's opener against the University of St. Thomas—Murphy got a phone call from Kirsten Teevens. It was important, she said, that he visit Buddy as soon as he possibly could.

"She never said anything about it being the last time I'd see him," Murphy said. "But it was apparent to me that was the message she was trying to send me, without actually saying it."

In forty-five years as a football coach, Murphy had never missed a single practice. He missed one that day. When he got to the hospital, he understood why Kirsten had called.

"He'd been fighting for six months by then," he said. "I had said to people right after the accident that it was amazing he had survived at all and that if anyone could come back from something like this, it was Buddy. He was such a competitor, such a fighter. But you could see that a lot of the fight had gone out of him. He was drained—physically, emotionally, and mentally. I knew in my heart that he really didn't want to live the way he was living.

"I could see why Kirsten had called."

A week later, twelve days shy of turning sixty-seven, Teevens died.

The entire league had already voted to wear "BT" decals on their helmets for the season. In New Orleans, all the counselors at the famous Manning Passing Camp, which Teevens had helped found while coaching at Tulane, had worn "Buddy Strong" T-shirts, as did Dartmouth's football players during pregame warm-ups.

"They didn't tell us all that much, but they didn't have to," senior long-snapper Josh Greene said. "We knew it was terribly serious. Even so, when they told us he had died, it was as if we'd been hit in the face. It was a very tough week." He paused for a moment. "It was a very tough year."

The team had already dealt with the death of teammate Josh Balara on March 16—the same day that Teevens had his accident. That had been a tragedy, not a shock. Balara had been fighting cancer.

The night that Teevens passed away, the entire Dartmouth football team—players, coaches, staff members, managers—gathered in the team meeting room that was used on game day for pregame prep. It was left to McCorkle to give everyone the news.

"As I stood up to talk to everyone, it occurred to me that every one of us in that room had been brought to Dartmouth by Buddy," he said later. "He had hired all of us as coaches, he had recruited all the players, and he played a role in bringing everyone who was in the room to where we were at that moment.

"It really hit me hard and I felt this huge responsibility being the one who had to give everyone the news. Probably the hardest thing

I've ever had to do. All I could do was try to channel Buddy: whatever we have to get done, we'll find a way to get it done. That's what he would have told us all. That's why I told the team: we were going to move forward. There would be no periods in our story. We were just beginning."

The home opener was that Saturday against Lehigh. It would be an emotional day, regardless of the outcome.

# Chapter Four

THE 2023 COLLEGE FOOTBALL SEASON opened on Saturday, August 26, in what the NCAA euphemistically likes to call "Week Zero." This is a way to hide sticking an extra week on the front end of the season without publicly admitting that starting the season in August was another way of adding a slate of TV games to be played in blinding heat by the "student-athletes."

Most teams began their twelve-game schedules a week later, the first Saturday in September. The Ivy League started two weeks after that—ten games in ten weeks. The opposite end of the spectrum was Navy, which played Notre Dame in Ireland in Week Zero and finished its season on December 10, playing in the season's first game and the season's last game, but with four bye weeks mixed in.

The Ivy League's first week was the only one in which none of the eight teams played a conference game—ranging from Yale hosting Holy Cross, which had been an FCS semifinalist in 2022, to Harvard playing a home game against St. Thomas of Minnesota, which was in its third season playing an FCS schedule after basically being kicked out of its Division 3 conference for being too good, having gone 55–1 in league play in its final seven seasons.

The weather up and down the East Coast was hot and sunny, with temperatures in the high to low eighties for the eight early afternoon kickoffs.

For two coaches, Sammy McCorkle at Dartmouth and Mark Fabish at Columbia, the openers were their debuts as head coaches. Neither had drawn an easy hand: they were two of three Ivies opening on the road—the third was Princeton, which traveled cross-country to play at the University of San Diego, the only game that would be played out of the Eastern Time Zone all season.

Dartmouth had to travel one hundred miles across New Hampshire to reach Wildcat Stadium at the University of New Hampshire. Columbia only had to go seventy-five miles to get to Fisher Field at Lafayette, but there was a lot more traffic from New York to Easton, Pennsylvania, than there was between Hanover and Durham, New Hampshire.

Columbia had finished 6–4 in Al Bagnoli's final season and the hope was the Lions could improve on that in Fabish's first season.

Lafayette was in its second season under John Troxell, who had played at the school and graduated in 1994. The Leopards had gone 4–7 the previous season, and most people expected a toss-up game, with Lafayette having a slight advantage because it was playing at home.

"If we both play the way we can, the game should come down to a play or two in the fourth quarter," Fabish said, standing on the field about an hour before kickoff. "Both teams have good defenses. The question will be which one can do a better job of making plays late on the offensive side of the ball."

The game started well for Columbia. After forcing Lafayette to punt twice, the Lions drove to the Leopards 24 before bogging down. From there, Hugo Merry kicked a 42-yard field goal for the first points of the season and a 3–0 lead with six minutes left in the first quarter.

"I was worried we might come out a little bit rusty," Fabish said later. "They had already played two games. That's part of the being in the Ivy League. The first week you are playing teams that have one or two games under their belt."

There was nothing rusty about the defense, but the offense looked a little bit shaky. Quarterback Caden Bell was missing targets, and the line was having trouble giving Bell the time he needed to get straightened out.

The real X factor in the game though was Lafayette running back Jamar Curtis, a sophomore who was listed at five feet eight but looked like he'd need a box to stand on to be that tall. Curtis was quick and strong—at times, he appeared to run under tacklers; at other times, he simply ran through them. Before the day was over, he would rush for 145 yards on twenty carries—do the math, that's 7.3 yards per carry—and two touchdowns.

The first touchdown came with 12:54 left in the half on a 6-yard Curtis run that put Lafayette in front, 7–3.

As it turned out, that was the last lead change of the afternoon. Lafayette scored again late in the half to take a 14–3 lead into intermission.

College football halftimes seem to last forever. They are supposed to be twenty minutes long but are longer than that because the clock doesn't start until TV interviews a coach or the teams reach their locker rooms.

The break is needed for about ten minutes, especially on a hot day, but, after that, everyone is just killing time. In most Ivy locker rooms, especially on the road, the offense and defense are separated from one another. For Fabish, the toughest thing about the visiting locker room at Lafayette was finding an area where he could talk and all his players could hear him. He reminded them that a fresh thirty minutes was still left to be played and it would be the Lions ball first.

"Let's go down the field and score and we can get the ball back and have the lead before the end of the third quarter," he said as his players crowded as close to him as they could get in order to hear him.

The Lions did get two first downs to start the half, but Bell was forced into grounding the ball by an all-out blitz on fourth-and-five from the Lafayette 45. Columbia forced a turnover but couldn't move the ball and punted. That was when Lafayette pretty much put an end to Columbia's hopes. The Leopards converted a third-and-ten from their own 20 with both punt teams ready to take the field. Instead, quarterback Dean DeNobile threw a 30-yard strike down the right sideline to Chris Carasia to move the ball to midfield.

From there, it took five plays to get into the end zone, the last coming on a dizzying 29-yard run by Curtis, who took the ball, cut left, and ran by the Columbia defense. The extra point made it 21–3 with 3:03 left in the quarter and, for all intents and purposes, the game was over.

Lafayette kicked a meaningless field goal in the fourth quarter to make the final, 24–3. As it turned out, the Leopards were much better than most people expected. They ended the regular season 9–2 (one of the losses at an eight-win FBS team, Duke) before losing to Delaware in the FCS playoffs.

At that moment though, it was difficult to know how good Lafayette would become. All anyone from Columbia knew was that they had been beaten soundly by a team they thought they could beat.

Fabish gathered his players on the field as soon as the handshakes were finished. "I love you guys," he said, a mantra he would repeat after every game, win or lose. "We weren't good enough today but we weren't as far away as the score says. We need to keep getting better, but there was nothing wrong with your effort and I know we'll be better next Saturday."

It is an unspoken tradition at most Ivy League schools for teams to gather on the field with their coaches before heading to the locker room—especially on the road where the locker rooms tend to be small. Often, players will greet their family and friends outside the locker room while still in uniform. Many visiting locker rooms don't have showers because they are much too small to fit the sixty-two players Ivy League teams are allowed to bring on the road.

"We competed," Mason Tomlin said later. "But that wasn't the goal. The goal was to win. It never crossed our minds we were going to lose that game."

In all, the league went 5–3 the first week of the season. The most surprising loss was Yale's to Holy Cross—not that losing to a team ranked fifth in the FCS rankings that week was a surprise—but the margin, 49–24 at home, was a surprise. The other loss was not surprising: Dartmouth, still trying to figure out who its best quarterback was, lost 24–7 to a New Hampshire team that had been 9–4 in 2022 and had reached the second round of the FCS playoffs.

Everyone else won. Harvard, despite Tim Murphy's concern about playing a team it knew little about, routed St. Thomas, 45–13; Cornell held off Lehigh, 23–20; Princeton made the trip to San

Diego look easy with a 23–12 win; Penn beat a solid Colgate team, 20–6; and Brown came from behind to beat Bryant—the school James Perry had coached at for two years—29–25. The only road winner was Princeton; the only home loser was Yale.

"We knew Holy Cross was good," quarterback Nolan Grooms said. "But we didn't expect that to happen."

Fortunately for Yale, one nonconference loss does not a season break.

A week later, conference play began with two games: Brown played at Harvard on Friday night and Yale hosted Cornell on Saturday.

Sadly, there was a moment of silence prior to each of the five games played in an Ivy League stadium that weekend. On Tuesday, September 19, Buddy Teevens passed away. The eight schools had already voted to wear "BT" labels on their helmets before the season started. Now, they all agreed to a moment of silence in Teevens's honor for the coming weekend.

It began at Harvard on Friday.

Every Ivy League stadium is unique, but none is quite like Harvard. Harvard Stadium is *not* the oldest in the Ivy League—it was opened in 1903, eight years after Penn's Franklin Field—but it *feels* the oldest.

There are no actual locker rooms inside the stadium—Harvard's players change in the football building locker room, which is about a 150-yard walk from the stadium. The visiting team changes in a double-wide trailer that is under the stands on the visiting side of the field. There is an entrance hallway in the double-wide that separates offense from defense and when the head coach wants to talk to his entire team, he walks back and forth between the two rooms so his voice can be heard by everyone.

There is also an element of danger in going to and from the field: Anyone over five feet tall must duck in order to get from the field to the locker room area or from the locker room to the field. Visiting coaches usually assign someone to stand by the entrance and say, "watch your head," as the players enter and exit the field. The Harvard players, once they are warned as freshmen, are more accustomed to "the duck." It is tougher on visiting teams.

In fact, in 2021, Alex Peffley, Cornell's director of football operations, was so intent on getting the players safely off the field that he forgot to duck and smacked his forehead so badly that the cut required a staple to stop the bleeding.

The Harvard players are also in two rooms with a small hallway between them. Murphy always stands in that hallway while his coordinators and various seniors give pep talks that are—to put it mildly—laced with profanity. Yes, Ivy League football players are often profane, though theirs is an eloquent profanity.

When it is Murphy's turn, the defense will crowd into the offensive side of the room and he will speak briefly. Then the players push the doors in the back of the room aside and everyone walks down the dank concourse that leads to the tunnel entrance in the end zone farthest from the football building.

The team will enter from there, stand in the end zone for the fight song and the national anthem, and then head for the sideline.

The Ivy League has had a Friday night package on ESPN since 2018. Every other Ivy League game is on ESPN+, the network's streaming service that was launched the same year that the Ivies and ESPN signed a ten-year deal.

The unfortunate thing for everyone involved—players, coaches, fans—is that the deal calls for TV time-outs to be taken whether the game is on ESPN or on its streaming service, which requires signing up and paying for in order to watch. The means that every game has sixteen TV breaks—not counting halftime—three in the first quarter, four in the second quarter, three in the third, four in the fourth, and four-minute time-outs at the end of the first and third quarters.

That leads to a lot of standing-around and sitting-around time for players and coaches, which grows more noticeable as the weather gets colder and on the many days when it rained early in the 2023 season.

Even so, the players love to play on Friday nights. It makes them feel special and, in the case of five of the games, they knew they were playing on national TV.

Brown-Harvard was not one of those games. It was played on Friday night but wasn't part of the TV package; it was on ESPN+.

Even though it was only the first game of conference play, it was massively important to both schools.

"We've been pointing to this game since last season ended," Brown wide receiver Wes Rockett said. "We're pretty sick of losing to them. And we *know* we're good enough to beat them."

Harvard had beaten Brown eleven straight times. In 2022 the Crimson had jumped to a 35–7 lead before the Bears scored three straight touchdowns to cut the margin to 35–28. Brown had driven the ball to the Harvard 38 before being stopped on downs with nine seconds to go.

"Don't think we haven't forgotten that," said Rockett, whose 17-yard catch in the final minute put Brown within striking distance at the Harvard 41.

The Bruins had gone 3–7 in 2022, with most of the losses close, like the Harvard game. James Perry was now in his fourth season as coach at his alma mater. He'd been a star quarterback on very good

Brown teams in the 1990s and had been the Ivy League Player of the Year in 1999 when Brown had gone 9–1 and tied with Yale for the Ivy League title.

He had come back to Brown in 2018 after two years at Bryant and, like most Ivy League coaches taking over a struggling program, had trouble his first three seasons—going 2–8, 2–8, and 3–7.

"We know we're better now," Rockett said before the team's opener. "We all learned a lot last year and we expect to go to another level this year."

One reason why the Bruins expected to be better was senior quarterback Jake Willcox, who had been injured the previous October in a win over Penn.

Rockett had grown up in Marblehead, Massachusetts, a suburb sixteen miles north of Boston and sixty-five miles from Providence. Rockett was a fifth-year senior because of COVID. He had improved each season. In 2019, his freshman season, he had caught two passes. After the year off, he had become Brown's primary receiver with fifty-six catches and forty-eight catches. Now, he was, without question, Willcox's top target.

On a brisk, overcast night, Brown started the game as if this was the year it was finally going to beat Harvard. Both of Harvard's quarterbacks from the 2022 team had graduated and the new starter was Charles DePrima, a junior from Ramapo, New Jersey. Among the three QBs competing for the job, DePrima was the best runner and had good size at six feet two and 185 pounds.

Playing his first prime-time game—literally and figuratively—DePrima started out tight, throwing an interception to Brown's Ethan Foyer on the Crimson's second possession. The Bruins drove 34 yards to take a 7–0 lead a little more than five minutes into the game.

After Harvard had to punt, Willcox and Rockett hooked up on a spectacular play, a 51-yard pass that Rockett, well covered, stretched and dove for at the Harvard 29, while being brought down from behind. It was a classic ESPN "top ten" play. Brown couldn't get into the end zone from there and Christopher Maron kicked a 30-yard field goal, making it 10–0 with twelve seconds left in the first quarter.

On the Brown sideline, there was jubilation. This was what they had waited almost a year for—and in Harvard Stadium no less.

Across the field, there was no panic. Murphy was coaching for the thirtieth time against Brown and he knew what a big game this was for the Bears. The team's attitude was perhaps best summed up by director of football operations Jackson McSherry who shrugged and said, "They always come out with their hair on fire against us. As soon as we get a drive going, we'll be just fine."

McSherry's words proved prophetic. Harvard put together a 75-yard, five-play drive that culminated with a 14-yard touchdown pass from DePrima to Shane McLaughlin to make it 10–7. One could almost feel the sigh of relief on the Harvard sideline.

Except that Brown promptly put together a drive that reached the 5 yard line with a first and goal.

Two plays then changed the momentum of the game completely. First, the Crimson put together a goal line stand that culminated when they stopped running back Nate Lussier inches from the goal line on fourth down. After picking up a couple of first downs to improve field position, Harvard sent in punter Sebastien Tasko to try to flip the field. He did more than that, landing a gorgeous punt inside the 10. It was downed on the 1 yard line. The field was officially flipped. Like a lot of punters do nowadays, Tasko took a phantom golf swing to celebrate the punt.

"Never played golf in my life," Tasko said. "Guess I should learn."

Brown went three-and-out and Harvard took over on its own 46. From there, DePrima ran the ball five times—with an incomplete pass mixed in—for all 54 yards, scoring from 3 yards out with fifty-five seconds left to give Harvard a 14–10 lead at the break.

As it turned out, Brown never caught up.

The offenses dominated the second half. Harvard would stretch the lead to ten; Brown would respond. Midway through the fourth quarter, the Bears cut the margin to 34–31, the third time they'd cut the lead to three points.

Harvard took over with 6:47 left and began milking the clock with short passes from DePrima to Cooper Barkate and with runs by DePrima and Shane McLaughlin.

College football had made a critical rule change prior to the season by taking away the clock automatically stopping on a first down until there were less than two minutes to play. That forced Brown to use a time-out whenever Harvard picked up a first down, the most critical coming when DePrima found Barkate for 15 yards on a third-and-ten from its own 43.

On the drive's twelfth play, the Crimson faced third-and-two from the Brown 22 with 1:47 left. The Bears were out of time-outs. The sense was that if they could get the ball back, even with no time-outs left, they would have a decent chance for a game-tying field goal.

With the Brown defense crowding the line of scrimmage, DePrima handed to McLaughlin, who burst through the line and had a clear path to the goal line. But a step shy, he went down on purpose—meaning Harvard could run out the clock.

"We actually practice the play for a situation like that," he said. "You score and they still have a chance to win—score, onside kick, score. It isn't likely, but it can happen. You go down, no time-outs left, you run the clock out with kneel downs. The game's over.

"Funny thing is, for a split second I forgot. Then I saw the goal line coming up and I thought, 'You better get down.' I barely made it. If I hadn't gotten down, I'm not sure I would ever have heard the end of it."

When he did get down, the game was over, except for kneel downs.

"I'm not sure Harvard people will understand what a good win that was," Murphy said. "They were a good team."

Most teams have some sort of postvictory ritual. Harvard's is unique.

While the team waits in the locker room, Murphy stretches his calves out for a moment on the steps outside the football building before walking inside. Once the signal is given that he's walking in, the players begin chanting, "Murphy, Murphy, Murphy."

He picks up his pace and is at full speed when he rounds the corner of lockers where his team awaits and DIVES into their waiting arms. He's been bobbled, but never dropped.

The "Murphy Leap" dates back to a win at Yale in 2013. Harvard had won "The Game," as their annual contest with Yale is known, to finish 6–1 in league play. Since the game had started at noon, it finished earlier than Princeton-Dartmouth. The Tigers were 6–0 and Harvard needed a Dartmouth win to tie Princeton for the league title.

As Murphy recalled, "We were dead stopped in traffic trying to get away from the Yale Bowl. [Police escorts are very rare in the Ivy League.] The kids were following the Princeton game on their phones. Finally, [tight end] Tyler Hamblin comes up to my seat and says, 'Coach, Dartmouth won, we're champions!'

"We weren't moving, so all the kids poured out of the buses to hug one another and celebrate. I looked up and they were all standing at the door of the bus yelling my name. I went to the door and they were all gathered there wanting me to jump into their arms. I had to show faith in my players. I took the leap and, of course, they caught me."

Since that day, all Harvard victories are climaxed with the Murphy Leap, but only after Murphy takes a couple of minutes to stretch his calves before entering the locker room. "I'm about to turn sixty-seven," he said the night of the Brown game. "I can't jump like I used to. I have to be sure I get a good running start before I jump. I don't want to fall short."

He hasn't yet.

# Chapter Five

IT HAD TURNED CHILLY AND rainy during the fourth quarter of the Harvard-Brown game, part of the remnants of Tropical Storm Ophelia that were sweeping up and down the East Coast that weekend. By Saturday morning, it was rainy almost everywhere and high winds were also part of the package.

Dartmouth's Memorial Field is the smallest of the Ivy League's stadiums with a capacity of eleven thousand. It fits well with the sign that is plastered across the length of the press box: "Welcome to the Woods."

As many Dartmouth grads will point out to you, "We're not on the way to anywhere."

And proud of it. "People used to use that against us in recruiting," Sammy McCorkle pointed out, looking at the sign on the morning of September 23. "We decided finally to say, 'That's right, we're in the woods and it's a great place to be.'"

Dartmouth was first established in 1769—the ninth and last institute of higher learning founded under colonial rule, and its motto is, "A voice crying out in the wilderness."

That's the way Dartmouth people see themselves. It has fewer than five thousand undergraduates and still calls itself Dartmouth *College*, even though it has a number of postgraduate programs. Daniel Webster graduated from the school in 1801 and, when the state of New Hampshire tried to take over the school, he argued the case to reverse that takeover in front of the Supreme Court, concluding his closing argument by saying, "It is, sir, as I said, a small college. And yet, there are those who love it."

That clearly holds true today. "It's almost like a cult up there," Tim Murphy said. "People go up there and they're part of the place for life."

That may help explain why assistant coaches rarely leave and why Dartmouth—on a percentage basis—has the highest rate of post-graduate contributions among Ivy League alumni.

Saturday morning was gray, and everyone assumed the rain would start sometime before kickoff. McCorkle and his coaches met with their players as they normally did in the football meeting room two-and-a-half hours before kickoff. Then, after the players left, McCorkle talked to visiting recruits and their families.

This is standard at Ivy League schools to meet with recruits on game day. Most big-time coaches are far too busy on game day for anything more than a hello-and-a-handshake for recruits. In the Ivy League, spending time with recruits is very much a part of game day.

Warm-ups were quieter than usual. There was very little of the normal pregame hoopla coming from the home team.

"It's a somber day," said quarterback Nick Howard. "There's no escaping it for any of us. The sooner we start the game, the better."

If anyone in uniform knew about dealing with tragedy, it was Howard. He'd grown up in Green Bay, Wisconsin, and had lost his mother after a long battle with cancer shortly after Teevens's accident the previous April. In a period of a little more than a month, he had lost a teammate (Josh Balara) to cancer, had seen his coach catastrophically injured, and then lost his mother to cancer.

"Actually, the only thing close to an escape for me was football," he said. "When I came back here after my mom passed away, my teammates and my coaches were here to help me get through it."

On the Dartmouth sideline, it was impossible to escape the tangible signs of tragedy. The players' helmets had a "BT" decal on them and a "JB" decal, too. On the bench where the offense would sit during the game, a green-and-white towel with Balara's number 76 was draped. Before leaving the field after warm-ups, many players knelt in front of the towel and, one by one, said a prayer in honor of their teammate.

Normally, when Dartmouth's players come into the locker room before a game, only those expected to play come inside. The locker room isn't big enough for the one hundred or so players in uniform, so those who are dressed for the game, but not part of the two-deep or special teams, wait a few yards away in the empty field house.

On this day, McCorkle brought everyone inside. They squeezed together, hands on one another's shoulders for a moment of silence. McCorkle took a deep breath and stood in the midst of his players.

He never mentioned Teevens's name. He didn't have to.

"All of you know he's up there today watching us," McCorkle said. "Here's what's most important for you to know: He's *already* proud of all of you for the way you've handled the last six months. You've all been amazing. He knows it, I know it. We all know it. He's proud of who you all are as people."

He paused for a moment to steady himself.

"You know he's looking down with that shit-eating grin that he gets when he knows everything is under control. He knows you guys have got this. And, when things go wrong today, which they will, just look up for a second and think, 'He's got this.' Because he does. He's still very much with us."

He paused again, still trying to keep his emotions under control. He moved to the middle of the room, his players crowding around him, put up a hand, and said, "BT Strong!"

They shouted it back.

There weren't a lot of dry eyes in the room, but by the time they took the field, they were clear-eyed and ready to play.

"We need the catharsis," senior long-snapper Josh Greene said. "It's been a long week. It's been a longer year."

After a terrible start—a 92-yard fumble recovery for a touchdown by Lehigh—the Big Green finally got some catharsis. In the next three-and-a-half quarters, they outscored the Mountain Hawks 34–3, before giving up a consolation touchdown late to make the final score 34–17.

The skies were gray throughout, but there was never a single drop of rain. The only person who got wet was McCorkle, who received a Gatorade bath to celebrate his first victory. Then, everyone lined up to sing the alma mater—a cappella—to celebrate the win.

As it turned out, Buddy *did* have everything under control. And, no doubt, he had that big shit-eating grin on his face.

McCorkle gathered his players around him in the field house before they headed into the locker room. This time, he didn't give a speech. He just looked up, pointed a finger, and said, "I told you he had it under control."

It started to rain about fifteen minutes after the clock went to zeros. Apparently, Buddy did have everything under control.

---

At Yale, neither Buddy nor anyone else had control of the weather. The rain was drenching most of the day and the winds made controlling the football difficult.

The game was important for both teams for different reasons: Yale was 0–1, having lost its opener to Holy Cross. Losing to a team that was ranked fourth in the FCS poll that week and had reached the semifinals of the FCS tournament a year ago wasn't shocking. Losing 49–24 was a surprise and a major disappointment.

Cornell had opened with a 23–20 victory at Lehigh and Coach Dave Archer thought playing at Yale would be a good measuring stick for how far his team had come and how ready it was to compete for an Ivy League championship.

"We'd gone 5–5 and we were very close to being better than that," he said. "We had our most important player [quarterback Jameson Wang] back and we had a bunch of kids who really wanted to make an impact in the league. Yale was a good test to find out where we were."

Archer was an upstate New York lifer and a Cornell playing and coaching lifer. He'd grown up in Endicott, which was about forty miles from Ithaca and had chosen Cornell over Harvard as a high school senior—a decision his parents are almost over. In case people wonder, he still has what Harvard calls "a likely letter," in his computer, telling him he's likely to be accepted to the school.

"I can't really explain it," he said. "It was just a feeling I had when I was on campus here. No doubt distance from home had something to do with it, but it was more than that. I just felt as if I belonged at Cornell." He smiled. "I still do."

Archer was an All-Ivy center at Cornell and, at forty-one, looks like he could still jump in the weight room with his players and bench-press a couple hundred pounds. He *looks* like a center with a blocky build and a round face that is usually creased with a smile—when he's not coaching.

Archer was Cornell's captain in 2005 and graduated with a degree in economics. He moved to New Jersey as part of the nonprofit organization Teach For America, teaching at both the fourth- and eighth-grade levels. He also worked as a part-time assistant coach that year at nearby Fairleigh Dickinson.

A year later, Jim Knowles, his coach at Cornell, asked him to return as an assistant. Five years later, at the age of thirty, he became the head coach—making him the youngest Division I coach in the country at the time.

Cornell has never been an easy job. Like Dartmouth, it is not easy to get to and its facilities aren't as plush as most Ivy facilities, which have been renovated or rebuilt in recent years. Archer knew that going in but was undaunted.

"We're the Ivy League's blue-collar school," he said. "We don't have any sort of indoor facility and our kids embrace that. They know we're going to practice in the cold a lot and they're fine with that, proud of it in fact."

Getting better had been difficult. The 5–5 season in 2022 was Archer's first nonlosing season. He knew that improvement on that record was almost mandatory if he wanted to keep his job.

"The way I looked at it," he said after the season was over, "was get better, stay, don't get better, and you're probably gone."

Yale, as the defending league champion and preseason pick to win the title again, was a good early test.

Wang, in his second season as the starting quarterback, was especially keen to be matched up against Yale's Nolan Grooms, who had been the Ivy League's Offensive Player of the Year in 2022.

"I think we're ready to play against Yale," he said. "I think I'm ready to play against their defense." He smiled. "And against Grooms."

Wang played with supreme confidence and with the kind of chip on his shoulder that was perfect for the Cornell mindset.

He was Asian American—his father was born in Taiwan, the son of Chinese immigrants. and his mother's parents were Korean. He had grown up south of Los Angeles, a very good student and a highly recruited football player. He had been recruited by most West Coast FBS schools and by the Ivy League but had chosen to go to Air Force, liking the idea of a tough, competitive environment and an option offense that would highlight his skills as a runner.

"I realized pretty quickly that it wasn't the right place for me," he said. "It was just too regimented. And the option offense they ran was completely different from anything I had run while I was in high school. It's a different animal. I should have realized all that sooner, but I had to actually live it to understand that.

"Plus, this was during COVID and with all the restrictions, it almost felt like you were in prison. By November, I knew the place wasn't going to work for me."

He dropped out of Air Force and took some time to decide where he wanted to go to next, taking prep school classes back home in Los Angeles.

While he was out of school, he worked as an Instacart driver to make enough money to have gas to make the one-hour commute to work out with Charles Collins, who had been his coach during his senior year at Oaks Christian High School. His father, Joe (who had played Division 3 college football), wasn't thrilled when he left Air Force and told him his expenses to commute the fifty miles to get to Collins were on him.

For a while, it looked as if he would land at Coastal Carolina. The Chanticleers had become a national story in 2020 when COVID cancellations made them a regular on national TV and they went 11–1, including a prime time victory over then-No. 13 Brigham Young when both teams were 9–0. Coastal, ranked eighteenth, stopped BYU on the 1 yard line on the last play of the game to hang on for a 22–17 victory.

Wang liked Coach Jamey Chadwell (now at Liberty) a great deal and was on the verge of committing to play there.

"But in the back of my mind, I couldn't stop thinking about the chance to play in the Ivy League," he said. "It was really Cornell or Columbia in the end and Columbia backed off me a little because, they said, my SATs [1210] were a little too low. I finally decided on Cornell. Calling Coach Chadwell to tell him I wasn't coming may have been the hardest thing I ever had to do. But he was great about it."

Wang has dealt with stereotypes since he was in high school. One was the old football cliché about height: he is barely six feet tall and, even in the Ivy League, that's short for a quarterback.

The other stereotypes are uglier. "I hear guys asking me at times how I can see down the field with my slanted eyes," he said. "It only seems to happen when I get close to the sideline and it's clearly only a few guys. Usually guys who *don't* play. The guys actually playing almost never say anything. I heard it in high school too. All it's ever done is driven me to want to be better."

Wang hadn't played at all in his first three games as a freshman, but a benching and an injury in the fourth game of the season—against Harvard—got him on the field. A week later, against Colgate, he saw extensive playing time off the bench and helped lead the

Big Red to its first win of the season. For the rest of the season, he played regularly off the bench and played an important role in Cornell's only other win, against Penn.

By the start of his sophomore year he was the unquestioned starter and the leader of the offense. "You don't have to be captain to be a leader," he said. "Especially when you're the quarterback."

Cornell's captains were offensive linemen Micah Sahakian and linebacker Jake Stebbins.

Stebbins had been calling defensive signals for two seasons and had been the defensive captain a year earlier. Although he had been scheduled to graduate in the spring of 2023, he had another year of eligibility because of COVID. Ivy League rules prohibit graduate students from playing (another silly Ivy League rule), so Stebbins had to drop out of school for spring semester.

Everyone respected Sahakian, but Stebbins was the leader of the team.

"We needed a lot more discipline in the locker room," Wang said. "Jake's brought that. No one wants to cross him in any way. He says do something, the guys do it."

The Cornell locker room has a big red "C" branded into locker room carpet. The players voted that no one—part of the team or not part of the team—would step on the "C."

"I don't worry about anyone violating the rule," Archer said. "I know Jake won't allow it to happen."

Yale had beaten Cornell in ten of their previous twelve meetings, and the Big Red hadn't won in the Yale Bowl since 2009. Cornell had never won an Ivy League title outright, tying for the title three times—most recently in 1990. The 5–5 record the previous season had been the first nonlosing season since 2007.

In short, Cornell had a lot to prove—mostly to itself.

"We know we're better this season," Wang said. "We're more disciplined. Two years ago we had a lot of guys who were playing for themselves—most of them seniors. Last year we made a lot of progress in that area. We were 5–5 but we could have been 8–2. We just didn't make enough plays at the end of close games. We were still learning how to win in tight situations. This season we fully expect it to be different."

It didn't start out that way. Yale was a ten-point favorite and it probably would have been more if the Bulldogs had played better against Holy Cross.

Grooms quickly led two scoring drives to give Yale a 14–0 lead. A Jackson Kennedy field goal just before halftime made it 14–3. Archer—as always—was blunt with his players at halftime.

"You're better than this," he said. "You know it and I know it, but now is the time we actually have to do it. Does anybody in here think we aren't good enough to beat this team? Of course not. If you go out and play like I know you can, I'll be fine with any outcome. But we haven't done that yet."

They did it right away in the third quarter. Wang, who would finish 16 of 26 for 226 yards throwing, led touchdown drives on Cornell's first two possessions. Twice, Cornell converted fourth downs—one on each drive—and when Wang threw a 3-yard touchdown pass to Nicholas Laboy, Cornell had the lead, 17–14.

Then, the defense dug in and made life difficult for Grooms, who would finish with only 117 yards passing on the afternoon.

In the swirling rain, moving the ball wasn't easy for anyone, but Cornell was clinging to a 20–14 lead midway through the fourth quarter.

There was no panic on the Yale sideline. The Bulldogs had been through enough close games a year earlier that they had complete faith in their ability to come from behind.

Which they did.

Grooms led a 75-yard drive that culminated with a 30-yard touchdown pass to Mason Tipton on fourth-and-20 to give Yale a 21–20 lead.

"Typical Yale," Archer said. "Just when you think you've got 'em, you don't got 'em."

There was still 3:20 left when Tipton crossed the goal line and Wang and the Cornell offense pieced together a drive of their own. The two key plays were a 22-yard pass from Wang to Doryn Smith and a 17-yard run straight up the middle by Gannon Carothers. Yale was looking to pass; Archer called run.

That play got Cornell to the Yale 27, well within kicker Jackson Kennedy's range, even in the wind and rain. Cornell began draining the clock and Yale was forced to use all its time-outs, hoping to get the ball back if the Big Red scored with enough time to have a chance to get into field goal range.

But Cornell was able to pick up one more first down on a third-and-one Wang run and, with Yale out of time-outs, Wang took a knee on the 20 yard line right in front of the goalposts and Cornell let the clock run to two seconds before Kennedy, who had already made two field goals, came out to try to make the winning kick from 34 yards out.

He drilled it as time ran out and Cornell won 23–21, its biggest victory in the Archer era and, arguably, as big a win as it had had in the twenty-first century.

"It certainly felt like it at the time," Archer said later. "The guys never blinked when we fell behind and Jameson couldn't have been cooler on that last drive. It's why he's a special player."

The day wasn't perfect. Midway through the third quarter, Stebbins went down with a knee injury that turned out to be a torn ACL. He was ruled out for the season, although he managed to make it back onto the field—and make a tackle—in the finale almost two months later against Columbia.

Stebbins was a huge loss, not only for his play but also for his leadership. He could still talk to his teammates and encourage them, but it couldn't possibly be the same with him wearing sweats on game day rather than a uniform.

On that dreary September day in New Haven though, the focus was on the victory; on the two comebacks—one from 14–0 down, the other in the final minutes—and on the stunning victory.

"I honestly thought we'd turned the corner," Archer said. "I thought that game was proof we could compete with anyone in the league. Unfortunately, competing and winning are two very different things."

# Chapter Six

As it turned out, the first week of conference play—two nail-biting games—turned out be a harbinger for the season to come.

A week later, when the other four teams played their first conference games, the outcomes were equally close: On Friday night, after being held without a touchdown for more than fifty-nine minutes, Princeton scored from the 1 yard line on a play so close it had to be reviewed, and beat Columbia, 10–7. And on Saturday afternoon, Dartmouth went to Philadelphia and pulled off a stunning 23–20 overtime victory over Penn.

That meant there had been four conference games in which the margins had been three, two, three, and three (in overtime).

"This is the way it is every week," Princeton linebacker Ozzie Nicholas said. "You have to understand that just about every game is going to be decided by a play or two in the fourth quarter."

Princeton had been a nonconference victim of that sort of game a week earlier, losing to Bryant—the same team that had almost beaten Brown a week earlier—16–13, in overtime.

"Just too many mistakes on our part," Coach Bob Surace had said. "You can't play that way here and win."

Penn was the third 2–0 team in the conference going into the third week of the season—along with Harvard and Cornell—having won at Bucknell and Colgate heading into its conference opener with Dartmouth. Columbia had emphatically bounced back from its loss at Lafayette to crush Georgetown at Robert K. Kraft Field at Lawrence A. Wien Stadium inside the Baker Field Athletic Complex. If nothing else, Columbia has arguably the longest stadium name in the country. Robert K. Kraft is the Patriots owner, who graduated from Columbia in 1963 and had given the school $5 million in 2007 for renovations and to have his name on the field. Lawrence A. Wien received his bachelor and law degrees from Columbia and went on to become a lawyer, real estate investor, and philanthropist; his lifelong donations of $20 million to his alma mater included $6 million for the construction of a new stadium.

There were two more conference games on that last weekend in September. On Friday, on a miserably rainy night, Princeton hosted Columbia. Then Dartmouth made the trip to Penn on what turned out to be a beautiful Saturday afternoon.

Columbia-Princeton was the first game of the official ESPN Ivy League package. That meant that Jack Ford was in the building doing the color along with his partner Eric Frede.

The case can be made that among Ivy League graduates today—outside of a president here and there—Ford is the best known.

He was raised by his mother on the Jersey Shore and figured out in high school that his best route to college was going to be football. He was recruited by Yale to play linebacker. He started as a sophomore—freshmen were not yet eligible—and was the team's captain in 1971, his senior year.

As a freshman, he watched in amazement and horror as Harvard rallied in the final forty-two seconds to tie Yale 29–29 after trailing 29–13. That game brought about what might be the most famous sports headline ever, the *Harvard Crimson*'s, "Harvard beats Yale 29–29."

Harvard's "victory" left the two teams tied for the Ivy League title. Both were 8–0–1 overall. That game was the last for quarterback Brian Dowling and star running back Calvin Hill.

"Still not quite over it," Calvin Hill said forty years later. "Maybe in another forty years."

Yale tied for the Ivy League title with Dartmouth and Princeton a year later, but this time it wasn't nearly as painful. Their only conference loss was to Dartmouth and they beat Harvard, 7–0, on a day when the Yale Bowl became a swamp.

Ford returned an interception 77 yards in a 21–3 victory over Penn that season when he was a sophomore and was a star from that point forward.

His first brush with television was when he appeared on *Jeopardy*, and won three times, helping fund his three years at Fordham law school.

He was a prosecutor for three years in New Jersey after graduating before starting his own defense practice in New York. Then, TV came into his life. He was hired by Court TV, when it launched in 1991, and later spent months covering the O. J. Simpson trial. He was hired by NBC as a legal analyst and became a weekend morning talk show host for the network. Ford has worked in various roles for NBC, CBS, and ABC. One New Year's Eve he joined Dick Clark for ABC's countdown to the new millennium. Seriously, Dick Clark.

But his real TV passion is Ivy League football. He's been the analyst on Friday night telecasts for various networks, the last six years on ESPN on the games that are televised by the network—six a year, five on Friday nights, always culminating with Harvard-Yale on the Saturday before Thanksgiving. Ford is seventy-three now, but looks fifty, which may help explain why *People* magazine voted him "Sexiest TV Anchor" in 1999.

He still lives at the Jersey Shore and makes the ninety-minute commute to New York, only when he has no choice for work. His house is less than a mile from the beach on a pretty corner in Interlaken.

Everyone in the Ivy League knows that Ford is a Yale graduate and he admits there are moments when he quietly shakes his fist when Yale makes an important play. But the coaches from the other seven schools trust him implicitly and appreciate what he does for the league.

"I'm not sure there's anyone who has done more for Ivy League football in recent years than Jack Ford," Tim Murphy, coach of Harvard, Yale's archrival, said. "He's always so prepared and his passion for the league is impossible to miss when you're watching a game. I think more people watch our games because of the job he does."

Ford doesn't make a big deal of his celebrity, but he enjoys every game he works. When Dartmouth and Penn held a pregame celebration of the fiftieth anniversary of the first game involving two Black quarterbacks, the host was Yale graduate Jack Ford. He does become a Yalie prior to Harvard-Yale weekend when former Yale players gather on Friday prior to the game.

"Everyone in the league knows where I went to college," he said. "But I think they all understand that I respect *all* the players and *all* the coaches," he said. "They also know that I do the games because they're fun for me, not for any other reason. There's no other league

I'd want to work in even if I was asked. I feel at home when I walk into any Ivy League stadium."

On the night of September 29, Ford walked into Powers Field at Princeton Stadium for his first Ivy League telecast of the season. The first stadium built on the site—Palmer Stadium—opened in 1914 with a Princeton-Dartmouth game. Eighty-two years later it closed—with a Princeton-Dartmouth game.

Palmer Stadium was demolished during the 1997 season. Princeton played all ten of its games that season on the road, including playing Yale in the 75,000-seat Giants Stadium in front of an announced crowd of 7,107. The new Princeton Stadium opened in 1998 and is easily the most modern of the eight Ivy League stadiums. The capacity, once sixty thousand, is now twenty-seven thousand, although it can be expanded to thirty thousand on the rare occasion when it is packed. The field was christened in the name of Earl C. Powers when he donated $10 million in 2007 to add FieldTurf and several other renovations. On a sunny day, it sparkles.

This was not a sunny day by any stretch. It was a drizzly evening at best, becoming more rainy and chilly as the game wore on.

One of the Ivy League TV rules is that all eight teams will appear as part of the TV package at least once a year. Years ago, this would have been an issue because Columbia was so consistently bad. In the forty-eight seasons, beginning with Aldo "Buff" Donelli's final season as coach in 1967 to Pete Mangurian's last season in 2014, Columbia had won sixty-eight conference games, had finished with a winning record twice, and had eleven winless seasons.

That began to change when Al Bagnoli arrived in 2015. Beginning in 2017, Columbia had four winning seasons in five and became known as a tough out for every team in the league. "They're very physical," Princeton coach Bob Surace said as his players ate their pregame meal. "Especially on defense. If you don't come in ready for a rock fight with them, you'll get beat up and you'll get beat."

Even with Mark Fabish now the coach, Columbia was still very much a Bagnoli team. The Lions were excellent on defense and probably a top-level quarterback away from being a legitimate contender in the league.

After the disappointing loss to Lafayette in their opener, they had bounced back to embarrass Georgetown, 30–0, in their home opener.

"As it turned out, neither of those games really told us who we were," Fabish said. "We weren't as bad as we looked against Lafayette and we weren't as good as we thought we were after Georgetown."

Princeton had been stunned a week earlier in a come-from-ahead overtime loss to Bryant. There was an understanding in the Princeton locker room that a loss in the conference opener wouldn't be acceptable.

"We have to be a team that finishes," linebacker Ozzie Nicholas told his teammates as the players ramped up before going on the field. "We didn't finish at the end of last season. We didn't finish last week. Tonight, we f— finish!"

Nicholas was one of Princeton's two outstanding linebackers, the other being Liam Johnson. Both were All-League caliber players—Johnson having been the Defensive Player of the Year in 2022. Both were team captains, although Nicholas was the more vocal of the two. He was hyperactive before games, stalking up and down the locker room once defensive coordinator Steve Verbit finished his X's-and-O's talk to the defense.

This was one of those survival-of-the-fittest games. It was comfortable at kickoff—sixty degrees and misty; but the temperature dropped and the rain increased throughout the night.

The defenses dominated for almost the entire sixty minutes. There was one score the entire first half: a 28-yard Jeffrey Sexton field goal after Princeton had driven 65 yards on fifteen plays late in the first quarter. That gave the Tigers a 3–0 lead at halftime.

That changed early in the third quarter. Columbia had gone three-and-out after recovering a fumble at the Princeton 43. But William Hughes dropped a punt on the Tigers' 9 yard line. On first down, quarterback Blake Stenstrom dropped to pass and, finding no one open downfield, turned to throw a quick swing pass to Jiggie Carr before he could be sacked.

But Columbia linebacker Justin Townsend read the pass, stepped in between Stenstrom and Carr, and intercepted the ball at the 2 yard line. His momentum carried him into the end zone untouched and, suddenly, with 12:08 left in the third quarter, Columbia led, 7–3.

"Against that defense, it was uphill from there," Stenstrom said. "I felt like it was on me to get it turned back around."

Stenstrom was different from most football players—especially Princeton football players. He was Princeton's first transfer since future NFL player and coach Jason Garrett had transferred from Columbia in 1988 after his father, Jim, had been forced out at Columbia after one (0–10) season.

He was also one of two married players—the other being wide receiver Connor Hulstein—on the team. He had met his wife, Hannah, in high school and they had continued dating when he went to Colorado for two seasons and then when he transferred to Princeton. They were married in the spring of 2021, and he had become the starting quarterback in 2022 as a junior. He'd been second team All-Ivy that season—behind Player of the Year Nolan Grooms—and was now very much the leader of the offense.

But trying to get going in the rain and against the Columbia defense, Stenstrom and the offense struggled.

It was still 7–3 when they got the ball back on their own 19 with 12:14 left in the game. "Plenty of time," Stenstrom said. "But the way things were going, it didn't feel as if we had that many chances left."

Which might explain why Surace twice went for it on fourth down as the Tigers grinded their way down the field. Princeton was mixing short passes with running plays and had twice picked up third down and long by the time it faced a fourth-and-six from the Columbia 29.

With the clock under five minutes, Surace felt like a field goal would do little good because his team would have to get the ball back and then drive at least into field goal range against a stubborn defense to win the game. So he went for it and Stenstrom, relieved not to see the field goal team on the field, found Luke Colella open over the middle for an 8-yard pickup to the Columbia 21.

Columbia dug in again and forced another fourth down, this one a fourth-and-two from the 13. Again, Stenstrom found Colella, this time on a short out route. Colella had to reach slightly behind him, but he made the catch—his seventh of the night—and was brought down just inside the 10. It was first and goal.

By now, just about everyone in the stadium—players, coaches, staff—plus the 5,107 in the stands—was soaking wet.

Three plays after Colella's catch, with the ball on the 1, Princeton had another fourth down with the clock winding toward two minutes. Columbia called time-out. When play resumed, Stenstrom handed the ball to running back John Volker, who pushed and wedged to the goal line—and in, barely—with 2:07 left, to make it 10–7.

It was the twentieth play of a drive that took more than ten minutes off the clock, remarkable given the way Columbia's defense had dominated Princeton for most of the night.

Columbia didn't give up. The Lions twice went for it on fourth down and picked up first downs and drove briefly into Princeton territory, but quarterback Caden Bell was sacked and fumbled with thirty seconds to play and the game was finally over.

While the Lions huddled around Fabish to discuss the near miss, the Princeton players charged to the locker room—in part to get dry, in part to celebrate.

Princeton's postvictory celebrations aren't random. They include a tradition that involves lifting one of the linebackers onto a chair—much like the bride and groom at a Jewish wedding—while he leads the team in two songs: "My House, Our House," and then the Princeton fight song.

In 2023, the chosen linebacker was Ozzie Nicholas, the ebullient kid from outside San Diego. The only problem with hoisting Nicholas onto the chair to lead the songs was that he was so enthusiastic it was possible he would knock himself out of the chair.

He survived though and was finally brought down amid hugs, cheers, and high fives. Princeton had won the game by—literally—one foot. And yet the atmosphere in the two locker rooms was miles and miles apart.

"Nature of the game," Nicholas said later. "If we had lost that game, I'd have felt sick, we'd all have felt sick. Instead, we all felt fantastic."

Soaking wet, but fantastic.

The weather finally cleared by the next morning in west Philadelphia, forty-eight miles away from Princeton Stadium.

The trip from Dartmouth to Penn was considerably longer—360 miles—a trip that took more than six hours in the rain on Friday.

No one was complaining, however. Exactly one Ivy League team—Princeton traveling to San Diego—would do so by airplane in 2023. Everyone else bused and no one bused farther than Dartmouth.

"All part of the Dartmouth experience," Sammy McCorkle said with a laugh, as he and his players walked in the direction of their locker room on a bright, breezy morning.

The sunshine was a welcome sight. It felt as if it had been raining up and down the entire East Coast in the wake of Tropical Storm Ophelia.

Penn Coach Ray Priore was also smiling when he walked into his office just off the south end zone that morning. He was dressed in a suit because the school was hosting a pregame reception in honor of former coach Jerry Berndt, who had passed away the previous December at the age of eighty-four. Berndt had only been Penn's coach for five years (1981–1985) but had turned the program around. After going 1–9 in his first season—the school's sixth straight losing season—he had gone 28–9–1 the next four seasons and had won two Ivy League titles and tied for two others.

No one would have blamed Priore for showing up at the reception in his game-day clothes, but Priore wore the suit. "It's a formal occasion and I'm representing the university," he said. "This is the right thing to do."

The game was the Ivy League opener for both teams. Penn was 2–0, having won at Colgate and Bucknell. Dartmouth was 1–1 after its win over Lehigh.

Penn's players were considerably more comfortable than Dartmouth's as they prepared for the game. The Dartmouth locker room was a typical Ivy League visiting locker room: just enough room for the sixty-two players with the lockers divided into rows so the players and coaches had to find a spot to gather closely together just before taking the field.

Penn's locker room, which had opened before the start of the season, was the Taj Mahal of Ivy League locker rooms. Priore had been able to raise $30 million to build the new facility, which was at the opposite end of the entrance to the field. The locker room had pods for each position and a row of comfortable armchairs for players to relax in and watch TV or game tape. Princeton's locker room was also comfortable, but not as large as Penn's.

"It's nice and the players deserve it," Priore said. "But once you go out on the field, it really doesn't matter."

Dartmouth quickly proved that Priore knew what he was talking about. After forcing Penn into a three-and-out on the opening drive of the game, Nico Schwikal blocked Albert Jang's punt, then chased it down and fell on it on the 1-yard-line. Quarterback Nick Howard scored on the next play and sixty-three seconds into the game, Dartmouth led, 7–0.

Dartmouth almost scored again a few minutes later. Running back Isaac Shabay fumbled for the Quakers and Sean Williams recovered at the 20 yard line. This time though, the Penn defense came through, stopping Dartmouth on the 16. Kicker Owen Zalc came in for what looked like a chip-shot field goal from 33 yards out, only the ball never got close to the uprights.

Joey Slackman, the defensive end and senior captain, who had come to Penn as a wrestler, broke through and blocked the kick cleanly. Suddenly, the momentum that had been all Dartmouth's changed.

It was hardly a surprise that Slackman would make a game-changing play. The surprise was that he was playing football. He had been the classic All-American kid growing up—captain of the football and wrestling teams at Commack High School on Long Island and a varsity tennis player. He had a 4.0 GPA and was a National Honor Society member in Spanish.

He was an All-County football player, but his best sport was wrestling. He won the New York State championship in the 285-pound division as a senior and was ranked twelfth nationally. He was recruited to Penn as a wrestler and arrived intending to wrestle.

But he still had enough of the football bug in him that he asked Priore if he could try out for football. Priore had never heard of him but he asked Penn wrestling coach Roger Reina what he thought. Reina said he thought Slackman was the kind of kid who would add to any team he belonged to. Slackman believed he could be a two-sport athlete and still thrive academically.

All of that came to a halt when COVID wiped out his freshman season of football and wrestling. By the time he was a sophomore, Slackman had decided to focus on football, in part because various injuries had hindered him as a wrestler, in part because he loved the team aspect of every play in football. He remained involved in wrestling by going to work for Beat the Streets, a program that taught kids from underprivileged neighborhoods wrestling and also tutored them academically.

He played in nine football games as a sophomore and by 2022 he was a starter and second team All-Ivy. "He's one of those kids you love to coach," Priore said. "You don't have to push him to work hard. He's just gotten better and better every year. He'll play somewhere as a graduate transfer next season and I think he'll have a chance to play at the next level when the time comes."

Slackman's block set up Penn's first offensive thrust of the game, a drive that stalled at the Dartmouth 4. Graham Gotlieb hit a

27-yard field goal to make it 7–3, but Dartmouth answered with a field goal drive of its own to make it 10–3.

Then, Penn quarterback Aidan Sayin hit receiver Malachi Mosley with a gorgeous 52-yard strike down the left sideline and the game was tied, 10–10.

But another Penn mistake, this one a fumble by Sayin as he was being sacked, led to a 36-yard Dartmouth touchdown drive, capped by a 14-yard pass from Howard to Chris Corbo to make it 17–10.

Yet another turnover led to a 26-yard Zalc field goal as time expired and, stunningly, Dartmouth charged to the locker room, leading 20–10.

Not surprisingly, McCorkle warned his players that there were still thirty minutes to go and that Penn would respond—especially at home. "That team over there has a lot of pride and they aren't going to make the mistakes [three turnovers, one blocked punt] that they made in the first half," he said. "You have to expect that they're going to rally and be prepared for the game to come down to the very end."

As he spoke, McCorkle paced up and down, in part because of nervous energy, in part so all his players could hear him. As he did, backup quarterback Jackson Proctor, who played often on passing downs, also stalked up and down.

"Sixth!" Proctor shouted. "They picked us sixth! What kind of BS is that? Do we look like a sixth-place team right now?"

Dartmouth had indeed been picked sixth in the preseason media poll, but given the tragedies of the offseason, it wasn't an unreasonable pick.

At the far end of the field, Priore was telling his players—though not in so many words—that perhaps those who had picked Dartmouth sixth *had* been wrong.

"We may have underestimated them a little," he told his players. "But that's okay. That's on us [the coaches], not on you. The mistakes are on all of us. Now, we have to dig in and just play better football."

They did exactly that.

The third quarter was dominated by the defenses, and things began to look grim for Penn when Dartmouth downed a Davis Golick punt at the Penn 1 yard line with a little more than ten minutes left to play.

But Sayin got his team out of the hole with a 52-yard strike to Bryce Myers. Even after another Sayin-to-Myers pass that would have moved the ball to the Dartmouth 5 was wiped out by a holding penalty, the Quakers dug their way out again, with Sayin finding Malone Rowley for a 16-yard touchdown that closed the gap to 20–17.

Dartmouth couldn't move again, and Penn drove to a second-and-one at the Big Green 29 with a little more than a minute to play. But on the next two plays, they threw an incomplete pass and lost 5 yards on a running play. On fourth down from the 34 with less than a minute to play, Priore sent Albert Jang in to attempt a 51-yard field goal.

Jang was the "long" field goal kicker. Anything up to 45 yards, Gotlieb was the kicker but on a longer kick, Jang who had a stronger though less accurate leg, came into the game. A year earlier, he had made a 51-yarder in overtime against Dartmouth to win the game. If nothing else, the distance was familiar to him.

Three hundred and sixty-four days later, his kick sailed right through the uprights and, with fifty-seven seconds left, the game was tied at 20-all.

Dartmouth went nowhere on its final drive and the game went to overtime.

Overtime in college football isn't like the NFL. Each team gets the ball at the opposition's 25 yard line to start. The coin toss decides who will get the ball first. Almost always, the team that wins the toss opts to let the opponent go on offense first: it is better to know exactly what you need to do when you get the ball. The longer the overtime goes, the more complicated the rules become.

Dartmouth won the toss and elected to defer.

Then, its defense came up big, forcing Sayin into three incomplete passes. On fourth-and-short in overtime, you might go for it since a touchdown puts so much more pressure on the other team than a field goal.

But on fourth-and-ten, Priore had to go for the field goal. Since it was 42 yards, Graham Gotlieb was the kicker. Gotlieb was from Boca Raton, Florida, and had come to Penn in large part because he wanted to go to Wharton business school. He was about as consistent as they came and had made a 35-yard kick to send the Dartmouth game into overtime a year earlier.

This time though, Gotlieb missed, the kick sailing just wide left. The Dartmouth players celebrated as if they'd won the game—which they hadn't—but their ebullience was understandable.

Even though his kicker was a freshman, McCorkle had complete faith in Owen Zalc, who was from Cary, North Carolina, and, at five feet ten and 155 pounds, looked more like a manager than a key member of the football team.

Taking no chances, McCorkle had Howard run the ball three times. He picked up 5 yards, clutching the ball as soon as he took off on each play.

On trotted Zalc for a 37-yard-attempt—having had one kick blocked earlier in the day. This time, he drilled the kick through the uprights and Dartmouth had a remarkable 23–20 win in a game in which it hadn't come close to scoring in the third or fourth quarters.

For Penn, the loss was stunning and painful, especially after dominating the second half. In the Ivy League, one loss is a big deal because, most years, it means you must win out to have a chance to even tie for the title. Penn had been 5–2 in the league in 2022 and that was good enough to tie for second place but not to share the championship.

For Dartmouth, the win was huge, not just in terms of the early standings, but emotionally. The players had vowed to be "Dartmouth" again after the disastrous 2022 season. Going 2–5 in the league and finishing tied for sixth place after three straight 6–1 seasons was unacceptable. Maybe that's why being picked sixth in the preseason rankled so much inside the locker room.

Add that to the tragic deaths of Buddy Teevens and Josh Balara and very much wanting the coaching staff to stay intact, and the Big Green had a lot to play for. Getting the victory over Lehigh at home four days after Teevens's death was a big deal. But winning the Ivy League opener on the road against a Penn team that was perennially difficult to beat was a much bigger deal.

McCorkle reminded his players that as good as it felt to win, it was just one game and there was still a lot of work ahead. But as he walked out of the locker room and left his players to celebrate, he had a wide smile on his face.

"It is just one game," he said. "But, boy, did that feel good."

He was entitled to feel that way. So were his players and his coaches.

# Chapter Seven

THERE WERE FOUR NONCONFERENCE GAMES on that last Saturday in September in addition to Princeton's Friday night win over Columbia and Dartmouth's stunning overtime win at Penn.

Two were walkovers for the Ivy League teams: Yale routing Morgan State 45–3, and Brown cruising past Central Connecticut State 45–20.

Cornell and Harvard both had far more difficult games. Cornell hosted Colgate, perennially an FCS power. The Raiders were off to a horrific 0–4 start but righted themselves at Schoellkopf Field, winning 35–25. That victory proved to be a turnaround for Colgate, which won six off its last seven games.

Coming off the massive win over Yale, the Colgate loss was a major letdown. "We knew they were better than their record," Dave Archer said. "They're always good. But we couldn't get ourselves where we needed to be all week. The letdown was predictable, but not excusable."

The best thing about Archer was his absolute belief in Cornell and in Cornell football. Even though he hadn't had a winning season in nine years, he believed his team was on the brink of being competitive in the Ivy League. He had seen the Yale win as proof of that. The Colgate loss was a setback.

"If you're going to be a good team, you have to be able to come off a great win or a bad loss and play well the next week," he said. "We didn't do that against Colgate. We should have been 3 and 0. That feels a lot different from 2 and 1."

The most impressive performance of the week came from Harvard. The Crimson traveled down the Massachusetts Turnpike to Worcester to play Holy Cross—not on campus at Fitton Field but two miles down the road at Polar Park, the baseball stadium that housed the Worcester (formerly Pawtucket) Red Sox during the summer. The PawSox had become the WooSox in 2021.

The stadium seated 9,105 and for football on a perfect New England fall day drew 7,920. Holy Cross had been a semifinalist in the FCS playoffs a year earlier and was ranked fourth in the country.

The Crimson knew their victory over Brown the week before was a solid Ivy League start, but they knew the Crusaders would be a more difficult challenge.

The first half was a lot like the second half of the Brown game, with the offenses dominating. Harvard scored first and led 21–14 at the break. Once again Charles DePrima was succeeding with both his legs and his arm. By the time the game was over, he had rushed sixteen times for 89 yards—and a touchdown—and had completed nine passes for 151 yards and two touchdowns. Five of the completions went to Cooper Barkate, who caught five balls for 73 yards a week after making the game's most crucial catch against Brown.

But the real heroes of the evening (five o'clock start) were the offensive linemen. Against a solid Holy Cross defense, they created enough holes to allow Harvard to rush for 209 yards—a little more than 4 yards a carry. Not only did this keep the offense moving, but it also kept the defense off the field against a team that had scored 49 points against Yale.

The defense got a giant lift from the return of defensive end Nate Leskovec, who had been overwhelmingly elected team captain the previous November. Leskovec wasn't as vocal as some of the other seniors on the team, but everyone looked up to him.

"Put it this way, when Nate talks, everybody listens," said offensive tackle Logan Bednar, a Californian, who might have been the most vocal player on the team. "There's a reason why everyone wanted him to be the captain."

Leskovec had been injured in preseason and had missed the team's first two games, standing on the sideline clearly upset he couldn't help his teammates. If you asked him when he'd be back on the field, his answer—through gritted teeth—was one word: "Soon."

He was back for the Holy Cross game, and there was no doubt that his presence on and off the field gave the Crimson a major boost.

Harvard never gave up the lead once it went up 14–7 in the second quarter. Every time Holy Cross got to within one score, the offense had an answer. When Holy Cross closed to 28–21 in the third quarter, DePrima found Barkate for a 31-yard touchdown to make it 35–21. An interception and a field goal made it 38–21, and Holy Cross's fourth-quarter touchdown to make it 38–28 was nothing more than consolation.

The locker room at Polar Park was small—built for a twenty-eight-man baseball team, not a sixty-two-man football team—but the players made room for the Murphy Leap. They were now 3–0 and ranked eighteenth in the FCS poll.

---

Harvard was the only unbeaten team left after week three. Princeton and Brown had won to be 2–1 and Cornell and Penn had lost to be 2–1. Yale was 1–2 and 0–1 in the conference, but no one was counting them out with six conference games left.

The Friday night game the following week was Cornell at Harvard. There's little doubting that Harvard and Yale are the Duke and North Carolina of Ivy League football. Some of it is that they play The Game the last week of the season, and even non-Ivy fans know that it is a big deal. Some of it is also that they are almost always good. Under Murphy, Harvard won ten Ivy League titles and, beginning with the 1999 season, he had more unbeaten seasons (three) than losing seasons (one) in his final twenty-three seasons as coach.

Tony Reno, his former assistant, who has coached Yale for eleven seasons, has now won four titles in the last six seasons.

Plus, Harvard is Harvard and Yale is Yale. That's no knock on anyone else in the Ivy League—in fact, Princeton almost always finished ahead of both schools in academic rankings nationally—but Harvard and Yale are Harvard and Yale.

As Archer had told me, Cornell likes to consider itself the Ivy League's blue collar school. It has no indoor facility for offseason winter practice and none of the players complain about that. In 2024, after Archer had departed, the school finally had enough money to break ground on an indoor facility.

"It's really part of our persona," said quarterback Jameson Wang, who is from California. "We tell ourselves this is part of becoming the toughest team in the league, which is what we absolutely want to be." Wang would be gone by the time the indoor facility opened. Harvard's facilities aren't exactly Alabama's either. Only Penn's Franklin Field is older than Harvard Stadium, by twelve years, but Franklin has undergone far more renovations through the years.

The lights at Harvard Stadium weren't installed until 2006 and they're still pretty dim—especially if you are watching the game on television. On the field and the sideline, they work fine, but there is a little bit of a twilight zone feeling when the sun is down.

Cornell arrived in Boston still reeling a bit from the loss to Colgate but confident that it could go on the road and compete with Harvard. Harvard had only beaten Cornell by a touchdown the previous season, and quarterback Jameson Wang was back, while Harvard had a new quarterback in Charles DePrima, which might—or might not—give Cornell an advantage.

Harvard's number-one goal going into the game was to keep Wang from picking up big yards running the football. The Crimson was willing to concede he would pick up yardage through the air but didn't want to give up big yardage when he ran out of the pocket.

They succeeded. Wang scored two touchdowns but only picked up 25 yards on fourteen rushing attempts.

"That's where he's most dangerous," Murphy said. "When he turns negative plays into positive plays. We have to control that."

In the meantime, DePrima, who had been excellent the first three weeks, had yet another big game. He only ran the ball nine times, but he picked up 152 yards and scored three touchdowns. He also completed twelve of nineteen passes for 209 yards and another three touchdowns, meaning, he totaled 361 yards and SIX touchdowns.

DePrima was from northern New Jersey—he'd played at Ramapo High School and was built like a quarterback: six feet two, 185 pounds. He had a good arm, but his main weapon was his speed. He had run the 40 in the low 4.4s and, once he had open field, was not going to be caught. *Maybe* in the NFL, but certainly not in the Ivy League.

With the score 7–0, DePrima started the second quarter with a 42-yard touchdown run that put Harvard in control, 13–0 (the extra point was blocked). Wang scored on a 1-yard run to cap a 75-yard drive to close the gap to 13–7, but Harvard and DePrima came back with a drive of their own, DePrima finding Scott Woods for a 36-yard touchdown and then following that with a two-point conversion pass to Tyler Neville to make it 21–7.

A 43-yard field goal as time expired in the first half by Jackson Kennedy, the hero of the Yale game, closed it to 21–10 and gave Cornell hope at the break.

"The emphasis has to be that we're good enough to beat these guys," Archer told his coaches before going into the trailer to speak to his players. "They played an almost perfect half. Now it has to be our turn."

Archer stalked back and forth between the two rooms, his voice raised enough that the Harvard players might have heard it on the other side of the field. That's Archer's way. He is emphatic when showing his players tape before they go on the practice field and he is emphatic at halftime of a key game.

Harvard was penalized three times on the opening drive of the second half and had to punt, but Cornell went three-and-out and Kennedy, who did all of Cornell's kicking, punted the ball to the Harvard 17.

It was at that point that the Crimson took over the game. It took them four plays to drive 83 yards to the end zone: DePrima to Tim Dowd for 45 yards; a 6-yard run by the always-reliable Shane McLaughlin; a 15-yard DePrima run; and a 17-yard touchdown pass from DePrima to Tyler Neville that made it 28–10.

That, for all intents and purposes, was the ball game. Cornell wasn't going to come from that far behind against the Harvard defense, and when the Big Red did get something going offensively, Harvard always had an answer.

Cornell did close briefly to 28–17, but DePrima went 58 yards for another score to stretch the margin back to 35–17. The final was 41–23, leading to a very happy Murphy Leap in the Harvard locker room. It was also the first conference game of the season decided by more than three points.

"They were just better than we were," Archer said. "We knew DePrima was good, but we didn't think he was *that* good."

The victory made Harvard 4–0, 2–0 in the conference, and put the Crimson where they were accustomed to being: at or near the top the top of the league.

The only conference game the following day was a 31–24 Yale victory at Dartmouth, Yale finally showing signs of being Yale for the first time all season. The four nonconference games were split: Princeton lost 12–9 to Lafayette. and Brown, surprisingly, lost 34–30 to Rhode Island. Columbia's defense pitched a second straight shutout in a 16–0 win over Marist, and Penn had to hang on to beat Georgetown, 42–39 in overtime. Given the Hoyas 30–0 loss to Columbia, the closeness of the game was a surprise.

The Quakers blew a 36–20 lead in the fourth quarter before scoring a touchdown in overtime to win the game after Georgetown had kicked a field goal on the opening possession of the extra period.

That made Penn 3–1 and in second place in the overall league standings. Remarkably, everyone else was 2–2 with only one more week of nonconference games. Beginning the week after that—October 21—the season would be decided by five weeks of conference games. This was the way it was every year: one week with all nonconference games; four weeks with a mix of conference and nonconference games; and then five weeks of conference play.

The rains came back to the East Coast on October 14. Everyone knew the Ivy League would be playing—again—in wet weather when the morning dawned.

Ray Priore was still in bed mentally going over what his team would need to do that afternoon at Robert K. Kraft Field at Wien Stadium to try to beat Columbia, when the phone rang.

Like most people, Priore tended to expect the worst when his phone rang that early. He was right. The caller was Michael Gavin Sr. His son, Michael, who had been diagnosed with brain cancer in June of 2022, had died that morning.

Michael was about to start his freshman year as an offensive lineman at Penn in the fall of 2022 when he was diagnosed. The cancer was untreatable, but Michael enrolled as a freshman and was part of the team throughout the season, even though he couldn't play.

"I never got to coach him, but he was a remarkable kid," Priore said, watching the rain fall inside the Baker Field Complex after his team arrived that morning.

The first person Priore called that morning was starting center Jake Bingham. Gavin and Bingham had gone to high school together and were roommates at Penn. They had stayed close throughout Gavin's illness.

"It was a shock, but it wasn't a shock," Bingham said later. "We all knew that Michael wasn't doing well. It was very hard to get that news on a game day, but I was going to go out and play the way I knew Michael wanted me to play."

It turned out to be the last game that Bingham would wear number 64. A week later, he wore number 62—which would have been Gavin's number—and kept it for the rest of the season.

Priore told the rest of the team about their teammate's death at their morning meeting at the hotel that day. It made for a pregame locker room that was quieter and more somber than most pregame football locker rooms.

The last thing Priore said to his players before they took the field was direct: "Let's be sure we remember Michael out there today."

The weather certainly fit Penn's mood: The rain was steady and cold throughout the day, with just enough wind to make it feel a good deal colder than the game-time temperature of fifty-four degrees. In short, it was miserable. Remarkably, the attendance was 8,032. It was Columbia's first conference home game and Penn's first conference road game. Both teams were 0–1 in conference play.

By any of its various names, Columbia's home stadium is remarkably pretty given that it sits a couple of hundred yards from Broadway and from the IRT subway. From the home sideline, one can see lots of trees, and behind the north end zone loom dormitories—not as attractive as the trees but a reminder that you're on a college campus.

Given the conditions, the quality of play was remarkable. There were only three turnovers in the entire game—one interception and one fumble by Penn and one interception by Columbia.

It was Penn's interception that set up the first touchdown of the game after Graham Gotlieb had kicked a 36-yarder at the end of Penn's first possession to make it 3–0. Rocco Milia intercepted an Aidan Sayin pass and returned it to the Penn 35. From there, the Lions needed seven plays to get into the end zone, with quarterback Caden Bell going 4 yards for a 7–3 lead.

Penn took the lead back midway through the second quarter, but Columbia pieced together a ten-play drive that culminated with a 1-yard Joey Giorgi touchdown run with twenty-three seconds to go. For the third straight game, Columbia had a halftime lead, this time, 14–10.

Both coaches said almost the same thing to their players at halftime: just the kind of game we expected. In a sense, these teams were almost cousins: Priori had been Al Bagnoli's assistant at Penn before Bagnoli left for Columbia; Fabish had played for Bagnoli at Penn and then been his assistant at both schools before suddenly becoming Columbia's coach in August.

The players felt none of that. All they knew was that they each wanted to come out of the rain with a 1–1 record.

For a while, it looked as if that team would be Columbia. The third quarter was scoreless. The teams traded turnovers and then punts before the Lions finally got a drive going late in the quarter. They reached the Penn 22, bogged down, and Hugo Merry kicked a 40-yard field goal to make it 17–10. At that point, Columbia's defense appeared to be controlling the game.

Understanding that his team simply couldn't run the football against Columbia's defense and that the wet weather and field made keeping up with the receivers' cuts difficult, Penn offensive coordinator Dan Swanstrom abandoned any pretense of trying to run and began dialing up pass plays for the offense.

Sayin was able to grip the wet ball and began finding his receivers on short routes, middle routes, and one deep route down the left sideline to Bisi Owens. That put the ball on the Columbia 4. After a penalty moved the ball back to the 7, Sayin found Owens again and the game was tied at 17–17 with 9:44 left.

One could almost feel the momentum cross the field from the Columbia side to the Penn side after Gotlieb's extra point sailed through.

Sayin was from Carlsbad, California—a San Diego suburb—and had been the starting quarterback since midway through his freshman season. He'd been honorable mention All-Ivy as a sophomore and was now one of the team's leaders as a junior. His brother Julian, who was three years younger than he was, had been the top-rated quarterback in the *country* for the class of 2024 and had signed with Alabama.

But in today's big-time world of college football, he never took a snap there. When Nick Saban retired at the end of the 2023 season, he became one of twenty-six Alabama players to transfer, leaving for Ohio State. Julian was the Sayin that people look at as a potential star; Aidan had to deal with none of that, being a very happy student *and* athlete at Penn.

After the Penn touchdown, Columbia quickly went three-and-out and Penn took over with a little more than eight minutes left. The Quakers began moving the ball and milking the clock, while the soaked fans on the Columbia side of the field watched in dismay.

A short punt set Penn up with the ball at its own 44. Sayin began completing one short pass after another and, on third-and-thirteen from the Columbia 31, he found Jared Richardson down the middle for 20 yards. That moved the ball from the edge of field goal range to well inside field goal range. Three plays later, with 3:04 left, Gotlieb nailed a 23-yarder and Penn had the lead, 20–17.

Suddenly, Columbia faced crisis only a few minutes after it had appeared to be in control. A penalty, a sack, and an incompletion, and the Lions had to punt with time running out.

They never got the ball back. Using their time-outs to hope to have some time after forcing a punt, Columbia never got to the part about the punt. Once again, Sayin found Owens on a critical third down, this one a third-and-four. With 1:38 left, Penn was able to repeatedly kneel down to run out the clock for a dramatic victory.

One team's dramatic victory is another team's devastating loss. Columbia easily could have been 2–0 in Ivy League play. Instead it was 0–2.

"Those are the games [Princeton and Penn] that you have to win to have a good season," Fabish would say at season's end. "In the Ivy League, you aren't going to win by blowouts or, most of the time, lose by blowouts. Games like that make a difference not just in the standings, but in your team's psyche."

In the Ivy League, it is a given that fans come on the field postgame. Unlike in FBS leagues, where fans "storm" the field (or the court) after big victories mostly for the purpose of taking selfies or getting on television, friends and family come onto the field after games to see the players and coaches.

Even in the rain, Penn's players and coaches lingered on the field to savor the victory. Bernice Bingham headed straight for her son, Jake, knowing how bittersweet the day had been for him. Jake had played a near-perfect game for the Quakers even with his mind on the death that morning of his friend and roommate, Michael Gavin Jr.

"I had to tell myself that for three hours I couldn't think about Michael after Coach gave me the news," he said, blinking back tears as his mom stood next to him with her arm around him. "It wasn't easy. There were moments when I couldn't help but think about what a great player he would have been for us if he had stayed healthy. He would have been a monster. Then there were other moments, even though I knew it was coming, that I just couldn't believe he was gone."

He forced a smile. "But I had to keep pushing all that aside because we *had* to win this game for Michael. We just had to win it."

A few yards away, Priore, with no apparent desire to get out of the rain either, shook his head talking about what Bingham had done that afternoon.

"Unbelievable," he said. "Just unbelievable. If the kid had said to me this morning, 'Coach, I don't think I can play,' I would have understood. Of course there was no way that was going to happen. This is a great win for the entire team, but what he did today is truly special."

The victory made Penn 4–1 overall and dropped Columbia to 2–3 overall. Remarkably, the season was half over.

"That's the thing about playing in the Ivy League," Joey Slackman would say later. "It feels like a marathon sometimes when you're going through it, but it's really a sprint."

It was the last weekend of nonconference play and the results were decidedly mixed. Harvard beat Howard easily (48–7) to raise its record to 5–0, and Yale also won with ease, beating Sacred Heart, 31–3, for a third straight victory. Not everyone was as fortunate. Cornell lost, 21–13, to Bucknell, and Dartmouth lost in overtime at Colgate.

The other league game went to Brown, which came from 21–7 down in the fourth quarter to beat Princeton, 28–27 in overtime—the Tigers' second come-from-ahead overtime loss of the season.

This one was especially crushing since it was a conference game. Both teams scored touchdowns in the first overtime, but Princeton's extra point was blocked and that was the difference.

"If you want to win the conference title, you can't lose a game like that," Bob Surace said. "All credit to Brown. They could have given up after we controlled the game for three quarters. It also helps to have a great quarterback."

Jake Willcox had a monster game for Brown, completing thirty-eight of sixty passes for 378 yards and three touchdowns. Mark Mahoney was the receiving star with nine catches for 153 yards and a touchdown. The yardage made Willcox the leading passer in the country in the FCS.

The outcome left the Ivy League in a complete muddle. Harvard still led the league at 2–0, but then came Brown, Princeton, Yale, Dartmouth, Penn, and Cornell at 1–1. Only Columbia, with two losses in games that easily could have been wins, was 0–2.

The season was at the halfway mark, but it was really just starting. Nonconference play was over. Now, everyone would dig in for the race to the finish line.

# Chapter Eight

ALTHOUGH YALE-HARVARD—THE GAME—IS BY FAR the best known and most publicized rivalry in the Ivy League, it can be argued that there is no rivalry more intense—hostile?—than Harvard-Princeton.

Some of this is simple: Harvard is everyone's biggest game. "We always have a target on our back," said Harvard coach Tim Murphy. "Let's face it, as great as all the Ivy schools are academically, we're Harvard, and everyone knows it."

That, plus the fact that Harvard is almost always one of the better teams in the league. Murphy had won nine titles coming into 2023 and the Crimson had finished in the top three on eleven other occasions. Their fourth-place finish in 2022 had been an outlier, only the third time in the twenty-first century that Harvard hadn't finished in the top three.

Murphy was the winningest coach in Ivy League history and was especially proud of his 19–9 record against Yale. But Princeton had proven to be a tougher out, especially in recent years. The Tigers came into the game in October of 2023 on a five-game winning streak against the Crimson.

"Officially they've won five straight," Murphy said. "As far as we're concerned, our last win against them was two seasons ago.

In 2021, both Princeton and Harvard arrived at Princeton Stadium with records of 5–0. The game was back and forth and went into overtime tied at 13–13. It was 16–16 after two overtimes, meaning, under NCAA rules, the teams exchanged two-point conversion tries—one play from the 3 yard line on each possession.

Harvard stopped Princeton's attempt in the third overtime, and then quarterback Jake Smith found receiver Kym Wimberly in the back of the end zone for the game-winning two points, making the final score, 18–16.

While the Harvard players celebrated, the officials routinely went to replay since it was a scoring play and it ended the game. There was no doubt that Wimberley had caught the ball inbounds. But, after a lengthy delay, the officials noticed Princeton coach Bob Surace trying to call time-out before the play started.

The officials decided to rule that the play never happened. When they informed Tim Murphy that they were granting Surace's time-out, Murphy was both nonplussed and furious. "You can't call a time-out after a play or because of replay," he said. According to Murphy, the officials told him he was right but *still* ordered the players back onto the field and put the score back at 16–16.

Harvard then scored *again*, but the play was called back by offensive pass interference. Princeton finally won in the fifth overtime.

The next day, the Ivy League admitted that the officials had been in error in granting Princeton the time-out after Wimberly's score. "The time-out should not have been granted and the play should have resulted in a successful two-point conversion," the league wrote in a release.

The NCAA rule book also clearly states that a time-out can only be granted between the end of one play and the ball being snapped for the next play, and there must be a visible time-out call made by the referee. None of that had happened.

Despite all that, the league couldn't reverse the outcome of the game once it was over. The only time there is any record of a result being overturned is a 1940 game between Cornell and Dartmouth when the referee mistakenly gave Cornell a fifth down on the last play of the game and Cornell scored to win, 6–3. When the mistake became apparent, Cornell forfeited the game, giving Dartmouth a 3–0 victory.

There is nothing in the NCAA rule book that allows for that sort of reversal to happen.

"I still look at that game as a win," Murphy said, standing on the field prior to the 2023 game. "That would have meant we were 9–1 and tied for the league title with Dartmouth. Instead, we were 8–2 and Princeton tied with Dartmouth. It still makes me angry."

He smiled. "And don't think I'm thrilled to see three guys from that crew here today."

There has been bad blood between the schools almost forever. In fact, they didn't play for eight years between 1926 and 1934 after a dispute over a fake *Harvard Crimson* story saying that Princeton coach Bill Roper had died. Roper, who is in the College Football Hall of Fame, had been ill but was very much alive.

There was also constant grumbling on the Harvard side about various college rankings, which seemed to often rank Princeton number one, MIT number two, Harvard number three, and Yale number four. How rankings like that are compiled no one really knows, but it rankled Harvard people that *anyone* would rank Princeton—or MIT for that matter—ahead of Harvard.

Harvard and MIT are neighbors and often play one another in basketball. The game is always played at Harvard since Lavietes Pavilion seats twenty-five hundred and has recently undergone renovations. Rockwell Cage at MIT seats about a thousand. As a result, a couple of hundred MIT students make the short trip to Harvard's campus when the schools play one another.

When the Harvard players are introduced, the MIT students chant "safety school."

"I'd like to get upset about it," Harvard basketball coach Tommy Amaker likes to say, "but it's so damn funny, how can I possibly get upset?"

That sort of humor is rarely on display when Harvard and Princeton get together—especially in football. It's worth noting that the call in 2021 didn't just give Princeton a victory, it helped the Tigers tie for the Ivy League title. All of which makes it that much more galling to Harvard people.

The Princeton people aren't exactly fans of Harvard either. They consider everyone from Harvard arrogant and condescending. In the Princeton locker room prior to kickoff, the battle cry was "To hell with ten thousand men of Harvard. Let's put ten thousand graves out there today!"

"Ten Thousand Men of Harvard" is Harvard's fight song, and it can be seen on posters all over the Harvard football building.

The day might have been the first Saturday in October with nice weather, although the weekend didn't start especially well for Harvard when one bus broke down en route from Boston and a second one broke down en route to the stadium.

That turned out to be a harbinger. The defenses dominated for most of the first quarter. Princeton's strategy was simple: don't let Charles DePrima have any open space to run. With his speed, he had controlled most of Harvard's first five games.

"If he was going to beat us, it was going to be with his arm, not his legs," Princeton coach Bob Surace said. "His arm was good; his legs were a lot better."

Harvard had taken over on downs at its own 43 with 6:45 left in the first quarter and had driven the ball to the Princeton 28. But Marco Scarano sacked DePrima for a 7-yard loss and, on the next play, DePrima threw deep down the left side to Cooper Barkate, but the ball was intercepted by Nasir Hill, who returned it 45 yards to the Princeton 48. A block in the back before the interception moved the ball into Harvard territory at the 42.

From there, it took tailback Jiggie Carr just two plays to get into the end zone—an 8-yard run on first down and a 34-yard burst up the middle on second down, putting Princeton up 7–0.

Princeton's defense continued to control the game in the second quarter. DePrima was sacked again and threw another interception and the Crimson never seriously threatened to score.

"We messed up his [DePrima's] season," said the always-blunt Ozzie Nicholas. "He'd been almost perfect until then. But Coach [Steve] Verbit came up with a great game plan and we executed it. We took away his speed and he got frustrated and started making mistakes. It was probably the best defense we'd played all year."

Harvard's defense was almost as good until the last possession of the first half. Taking over at midfield after a short punt, quarterback Blake Stenstrom completed three straight passes to get the ball to the Harvard 12 with under a minute to go. Even after a penalty pushed the ball back to the 30, Stenstrom continued to attack and, finally, with the ball on the 8 and third down, he found AJ Barber in the right corner of the end zone with thirty-six seconds left for a touchdown that made it 14–0 at halftime.

Murphy isn't a screamer, regardless of score, but he made it clear to his players that he wasn't very happy with the first thirty minutes.

"I think we'd all agree that this is the first time all season we've faced any real adversity," he said. "Well, now we get to find out how we deal with adversity. Do we just fold up because things haven't gone well, because we've made some mistakes we shouldn't make? Or do we find out what kind of team we have? I know what kind of team I think we have. Let's go out and *show them* what kind of team we have."

Easier said than done. The defenses continued to dominate in the third quarter. The Tigers simply refused to give DePrima any room to operate when he tried to run. Only running back Shane McLaughlin—twelve carries for 65 yards—was able to pick up any yardage on the ground. At the same time, the Harvard defense shut down the Princeton offense.

Finally, late in the third quarter, the Crimson began to move the ball. McLaughlin rushed the ball three straight times to get the ball into Princeton territory. Then, DePrima finally hit a long pass, finding Kaedyn Odermann down the right sideline to the 11 yard line. Three plays after that, he found Odermann again, this time for a touchdown. With ten seconds left in the third quarter, Harvard was finally on the board, and it was 14–7.

The momentum had clearly changed. The Princeton bench was as quiet as it had been all day. The Harvard sideline was very much alive, especially when the Tigers quickly went three-and-out. It was the Tigers' fourth straight three-and-out of the half. A short punt and a fair catch interference penalty gave Harvard the ball at the Princeton 38, and the Crimson moved methodically from there—ten plays on the ground, except for one incomplete pass leading to McLaughlin's 1-yard run that tied the score at 14 with 9:40 left in the game.

If nothing else, Murphy had found out what kind of team he had.

Princeton finally picked up a first down after the kickoff. Harvard stopped the Tigers on their 41 yard line, but punter Brady Clark then dropped a perfect kick on the Harvard 3 yard line. That play turned out to be critical. A key delay-of-game penalty forced a punt, and punter Sebastien Tasko got off a rare poor punt, the ball going out of bounds after just 30 yards, giving Princeton the ball back at the Harvard 45 with 4:02 left.

A 15-yard pass over the middle got the Tigers into field goal range and they began draining the clock. Harvard took a time-out with 1:41 left hoping to have enough time to answer the field goal that seemed inevitable. But on third down from the 10 yard line, Stenstrom fooled the Harvard defense, which was expecting a run to take more time off the clock. He dropped back and found Connor Hulstein open on the left side. Hulstein dove into the end zone with 1:25 left and, suddenly, stunningly, Harvard needed a touchdown to tie when the extra point made it 21–14.

It may also have been the first critical touchdown pass in Ivy League history from one married player to another married player.

The Crimson then went nowhere after the kickoff. DePrima was sacked for a 9-yard loss and then, desperate, threw a pass into coverage that was intercepted by Will Perez at the Harvard 37. It was the third interception DePrima had thrown. Two kneel-downs by Stenstrom ran out the clock. Final: Princeton 21, Harvard 14.

Princeton's victory created chaos in the Ivy League race. If Harvard had won, it would have been 3–0 with everyone chasing. Princeton's hopes would pretty much have gone up in smoke at 1–2. Instead, Princeton was 2–1 and tied for first with Harvard, surprise teams Dartmouth and Cornell, and Penn. The Big Green had won at home against Columbia 20–9, and the Big Red had bounced back after the loss to Harvard and had routed Brown, 36–14, also at home.

Jameson Wang, who had been passed on by Princeton and Columbia because coaches had doubts about his throwing arm, threw for 330 yards and two touchdowns. The fourth game of the day produced a minor upset, Penn going into the Yale Bowl and beating the Eli, 27–17. That dropped Yale to 1–2 in the league along with Brown. Columbia, after yet another close loss, was 0–3.

Penn's victory was a surprise because it seemed as if Yale had turned things around after its 0–2 start. "We lost because Penn played well and we didn't play well," Yale coach Tony Reno said with a shrug a few days later. "In this league, it's pretty simple: if you don't play well, you lose. I look at the rest of our schedule and I honestly believe we can win all four games. I also believe we can lose all four games. The league is that evenly matched. If our guys look at Columbia's record coming in here this week and think, 'That's a win,' I guarantee you we won't win."

The celebration at Princeton after the Harvard win was raucous. The only nonraucous moment came when the players got a little out of control after lifting Nicholas to lead the two victory songs. Instead of moving to the middle of the locker room where the ceiling was highest, they moved in the direction of the opening between lockers that led to one of the locker room doors and his head came dangerously close to the ceiling.

"Watch out, watch out!" Surace screamed, semi-panicked. Whether anybody heard him was hard to say but Nicholas's head came within a couple of inches of the ceiling.

"Never noticed," Nicholas said later. "I was too busy singing."

Surace breathed a sigh of relief when the singing ended and Nicholas was safely back on the ground.

"That's not the way you want to lose an All-Ivy linebacker," he said, able to laugh when Nicholas was in one piece.

The tradition of lifting a linebacker to lead the two songs had been started by Roger Hughes when he took over as coach in 2000. Initially, one of the linebackers would jump on a table in the locker room and lead everyone in "Our House, My House!" and then in the Princeton fight song.

"It had to be a linebacker because the linebackers are the leaders and the voices of the defense," said defensive coordinator Steve Verbit, who had been on the staff since 1985. "It has always been up to the linebackers who would lead the songs."

The tradition had evolved to singing the songs on the field after road wins and then to the selected linebacker being lifted on his teammates' shoulders outdoors and onto a chair indoors.

Since fellow linebacker Liam Johnson had been the Ivy League's Defensive Player of the Year as a junior, Nicholas and everybody else had figured he would be the lead singer in 2023. But the Tigers had opened the season in San Diego—Nicholas's hometown. "I would say at least 20 percent of the people in the Princeton section were my friends and family," he said. "I had a really good game and we won so Liam just said to me, 'You do the songs,' afterwards and it made sense, so I said okay."

Two weeks later, after the tense victory over Columbia, Nicholas assumed it would be Johnson who would lead the songs. But when they got into the locker room, the two roommates began to argue about who would be going up in the air.

"I just figured it should be him," Nicholas said. "But, being honest, that's not really Liam's sort of thing. We argued until the last possible second and, finally, he just said, 'You're doing it,' and the next thing I knew, everyone had me up in the air."

Nicholas may have wanted his buddy to be the one leading the song, but he didn't hate doing it. "No, I didn't hate it," he said with a grin. "I just wish we had been able to do it more often."

After the win over Harvard, the Princeton players honestly believed they had as good a chance to win out as anyone else in the league.

There were five teams—Harvard, Princeton, Cornell, Dartmouth, and Penn—tied for first place at 2–1. Yale and Brown were 1–2 with Columbia 0–3.

Chaos indeed.

About an hour before the Harvard-Princeton kickoff, Princeton coach Bob Surace sat relaxing on his team's offensive bench. He had walked the field already, saying hello to Tim Murphy, most of Harvard's assistants, and the seven officials. Unlike in FBS leagues, the Ivy League uses a seven-man, on-field officiating crew in order to save a few dollars. The officials are well-paid—$1,250 per game—but the schools choose to save money by using one less official.

Once he'd walked the field, Surace sat on one of his team's benches and spoke to just about anyone who wandered nearby. He'd already spoken to visiting recruits and their family's at a reception that included players and coaches to familiarize the players with the coaches they would be playing for if they came to Princeton.

Now, while the visitors wandered the sidelines as the teams warmed up, Surace greeted others: staff, media, sponsors, and NFL scouts.

An outsider might be surprised by the number of scouts who show up at Ivy League games. In 2022, there were fourteen Ivy Leaguers on NFL rosters—quite a few more than most people might expect.

Ivy League players are valued by NFL teams because—generally speaking—they're smart, they're willing to work hard to continue their football careers beyond college, and they're good teammates.

On this day, a slew of scouts greeted Surace and, after a minute or two of small talk, asked the same question: "How's 71?"

Scouts often refer to players by number rather than name. It's more a football-jock thing; coaches often do it too—but for the scouts it makes it easier than remembering names. In this case, "71" was Jalen Travis, and he was one of the few players who the scouts could easily identify without a number on his back.

Travis was six feet seven and weighed 315 pounds. He was a classic All-American kid—great grades, a future that went way beyond football, and the kind of personality that made you instantly like him.

"He'll be a senator someday—at least," quarterback Blake Stenstrom said. "He just has it all."

The only thing Travis lacked that day was health. He had been injured in the Bryant game when someone fell on his knee while he was making a third-quarter tackle.

"At first it didn't feel too bad," he said. "But when I was coming off the field, I could feel something loose in my knee. I didn't think it was an ACL, but I knew something was wrong."

He was right on both counts—his ACL was okay, but he had hurt his MCL. Unlike the ACL, which is almost always season-ending, the length or recovery time for an MCL injury can vary from very little time to season-ending.

Travis was smack in the middle. He knew he'd be out a couple of weeks but hoped that would be it. Only it wasn't. He had hoped to return after missing two games, but he wasn't ready to go against Brown, a game Princeton lost 28–27 in overtime with Travis pacing up and down the sideline with a crutch under his right arm.

"Next week," he said. "Has to be next week."

Only it wasn't.

He practiced the following week and thought he was ready to play. But during warm-ups, the knee still felt loose and he was having trouble pushing off. "If I can't push off, I can't be effective," he said. "I couldn't believe it. But I didn't want to hurt the team by playing and being ineffective."

He finally sat down to let the trainers and doctors look at the knee. They advised him to wait one more week—which was heartbreaking.

"It was our biggest game of the year," he said. "I couldn't believe I wasn't going to play. But I knew it was the right thing for the team."

Travis had grown up in Minneapolis and was the fourth of Nate and Jackie Travis's five children. His dad was Black; his mom was White. His older brother, Jonah, had played at Harvard. Jalen seriously considered Harvard but didn't want to feel as if he was playing in Jonah's shadow.

He had been recruited by both Iowa and Minnesota but wanted to play in the Ivy League.

"I really liked the Princeton coaches," he said. "They never said a bad word about any other schools that were recruiting me. They didn't tell me what other schools didn't have, but what Princeton *did* have. I was completely comfortable with them right away."

He played part-time as a freshman in 2019 and was home in Minneapolis on May 25, 2020, when George Floyd was murdered not far from his home. As was the case for many people, he was deeply affected by the murder and the viral video of police officer Derek Chauvin pressing his knee onto Floyd's neck even while Floyd was pleading for mercy.

"It was just so horrifying to watch," Travis said. "A police officer committing murder while other cops stood and watched. I just felt I had to do something, not just say, 'This is wrong.' It was beyond wrong."

Travis and a high school buddy, Matthew Seroud, formed the Just Action Coalition, a group made up of young activists who wanted to recruit people to become more involved in policy and poverty issues. The formation of the group was one of the reasons that Travis won a Truman Scholarship Award at the end of the 2023 school year, a $30,000 postgraduate scholarship award given to one student in each state. Prior to that, he was an intern in Washington for Minnesota senator Amy Klobuchar. His hope all along has been to go to law school and practice public policy law.

Short term though, Travis just wanted to play football. Finally, a week after the Harvard game, he got back on the field, at Cornell. The Tigers beat the Big Red, 14–3, that day, improving their record to 3–1 in the league. That tied them for the league lead with Harvard. Everyone else, except for Columbia, was a game back at 2–2.

All seven of those teams remained convinced they could be league champions as October turned to November and the weather began to cool.

# Chapter Nine

PRINCETON'S VICTORY OVER HARVARD MAY have raised the most eyebrows around the Ivy League in week six of the season, but it was not the most surprising outcome that day.

In all, it was a good week for home teams. In addition to Princeton's victory, Dartmouth beat Columbia 20–9 at Memorial Field and Cornell beat Brown 38-14, a surprising margin of victory.

But the biggest surprise was the one victory for a visitor. Just when it appeared that Yale had put its 0–2 start behind it, the Bulldogs were beaten by Penn 27–17 before a shocked crowd of 3,817 in the Yale Bowl. Penn's defense did a superb job of keeping Yale quarterback Nolan Grooms under control—he threw for only 121 yards and one interception while rushing for 60 yards, an off-day for him. In the meantime, Penn quarterback Aidan Sayin had, arguably, his best day of the season completing thirty-three of forty-eight passes for 364 yards and two touchdowns.

"Looking back, that had to be our best game of the season," Coach Ray Priore said. "Aidan was terrific, we didn't turn the ball over, and both our lines were excellent. Beating Yale or Harvard is a big deal in this league. I was really proud of my guys that day."

With four weeks left in the season, there were five teams tied for first place with records of 2–1: Harvard, Princeton, Penn, Dartmouth, and Cornell. Yale and Brown were 1–2 and Columbia was 0–3. That meant seven of the eight teams were within a game of first place.

"That's the way this league is most of the time," Yale coach Tony Reno said. "It isn't just that the standings are close, it's that the *games* are close. I go into every league game figuring a play or two will decide the game.

"Last week was an exception. They won because they played well. We lost because we didn't play well. They deserved to win. We deserved to lose. It was that simple."

Reno was sitting behind a desk in one of the trailers that was the game-day headquarters for the Bulldogs during the 2023 season while the 109-year-old Yale Bowl was being renovated.

This was a less-than-ideal year for renovations. Ivy League teams normally play five home games, occasionally six. Yale had seven home games—four in conference, three nonconference. In 2024 when the renovation was (presumably) complete, it would have five home games.

"It's just the way the schedule broke," Reno said. "Not ideal, but we're handling it."

As emotional as he might be on the sideline, Reno is almost always low-key away from it. When the subject of the Penn game came up, Reno shrugged matter-of-factly. "We weren't unlucky, we just didn't play well enough to win. We *do* have a bunch of linemen with injuries, more than most years, but everyone has injuries."

Depth is very important in the Ivy League because most teams don't have that much of it. If a player feels he can play regularly at an Ivy League school, he might very well choose to go there, knowing he will get an excellent education. If he has NFL talent, he will be seen by NFL scouts.

But if someone doesn't think of himself as a pro prospect and isn't recruited very much by the Ivies, he might choose an academically oriented Division 3 school, knowing he will get a chance to play and get a good education. On the rare occasion when a D-3 player lands in the NFL, it is because he grew in college or improved greatly during that period.

Most Ivy League backups are kids who hope to get more playing time as their careers move forward. Some do.

Brown wide receiver Wes Rockett had two catches for 42 yards as a freshman. As a senior, he had 71 catches for 794 yards and a total of five touchdowns.

Yale quarterback Nolan Grooms threw a total of five passes as a freshman. He became the starter as a sophomore and threw for more than 5,000 yards the next three seasons and was the Ivy League Offensive Player of the Year as a junior and senior.

Football, especially at the Ivy League level, is usually dominated by juniors and seniors who work at their craft all year round and get better. Joey Slackman, the walk-on who had originally arrived on campus to wrestle, was the Defensive Player of the Year in 2023 and will be a grad transfer at Florida in 2024. He chose Florida from among thirty FBS schools that actively recruited him and is considered to be a legitimate NFL prospect.

The other noticeable difference between most Ivy League players and FBS powers is size: At six feet seven and 315 pounds, Jalen Travis stands out like a lighthouse in a storm on the sidelines.

Standing on the sideline during Ivy League games, it is impossible not to notice the size—or lack of it—among most players. I'm six feet tall and often I noticed players standing next to me who were my height or close to it—and I'm not talking about kickers.

What the best Ivy players have are smarts and work ethic. Logan Bednar, Harvard's starting right tackle, played very little for most of his first three years. As a senior, he was not only a starter in all ten games but also one of the team's spiritual and most vocal leaders.

"It's funny because it took me a long time to be a starter; I'm not the captain [Nate Leskovec was the '23 captain] and I'm not even our best offensive lineman," he said. "That's Jacob Rizy. But I know my role with this team, and there's nothing I won't do to fill that role."

Captain or not, when Bednar spoke, his teammates listened. He was always the first offensive player to stand up in front of the team in the pregame locker room. He would walk to the front of the room with a big grin on his face. He talked the usual trash that you talk about an opponent and the fact that they had *no chance* to beat the Crimson.

But the focus of his talks was almost always about his teammates and his coaches. He would single out certain players and how much faith he had in each of them and how he *knew* how good they were individually and as a group. By the time he was finished, everyone in the room was ready to break down the doors and charge the field: Players, coaches—hell, reporters. He was that good.

Leskovec, who had grown up in Solon, Ohio, was different. His emotion would build as he spoke, and the respect for him was so great that the room was deadly quiet while he spoke.

"Nate is *the* leader of his team," Bednar said. "We all know that. He's more the leader by example. I'm more a leader by profanity."

Bednar combined humor (and profanity) in conveying reasons to dislike the opponent; reasons to honor wearing the Harvard uniform; a joke or two—usually directed at the opponent—and how important it was for Harvard to win *this game.*

"It helped that I only had to come up with ten rants," he said with a smile.

Others would follow—notably Rizy on the offensive side and Leskovec on the defensive side. When the players were finished, Murphy would step in with what was usually a brief speech that would end with everyone kneeling to say the Lord's Prayer. Then it was time to go play.

Ivy League players know that no matter where they are on the depth chart in August, they might very well find themselves starting in October and November.

There was no better example of that than Yale. On the day of the Columbia game, no fewer than eleven players were on crutches. This was especially difficult because to get to the field from the nonlocker rooms, one had to go down a flight of fourteen steps and then down a ramp—and then repeat that trip going uphill to get back to the rooms at halftime. No one complained.

This was a crossroads game for both teams. Yale was 3–3 overall and 1–2 in conference play. Columbia was 2–4 and 0–3—losing to Princeton and Penn by three points and at Dartmouth the previous week, 20–9. Yale still had a slim chance to compete for the conference title; Columbia was hoping it could turn close losses into close wins and still finish over .500. Interim Coach Mark Fabish suspected that if he wanted the "interim" tag removed from his title, his team would have to win at least three of its remaining four games

The last Saturday in October in New Haven was spectacular. It was 71 degrees and sunny at kickoff with almost no wind. A fairly typical non–Yale-Harvard Ivy League crowd of 5,422 rattled around the old stadium, watching what turned out to be one of the season's most one-sided conference games.

"Funny thing is, we've got four games left, and I honestly believe we can win all four of them and still have a chance to at least tie for the title," Reno said a couple of hours before kickoff. "But we could also lose all four depending on the way we play."

Yale's players and coaches had put a good deal of emphasis on winning a second straight title during preseason. In fact, that had been a recurring theme when they talked about where their motivation would come from once the season started. After the season was over, Reno wondered if that had been a mistake.

"We'd never won two in a row since I got here," he said. "We went 9–1, then 5–5; then 9–1 followed by 5–5 again. Last year we were 8–2 and, especially with a lot of key guys back, going 5–5 wasn't going to be acceptable. Our goal was to go back-to-back because Yale hadn't done that since 1981."

That season, Yale had won a third straight title, tying with Dartmouth after winning the league outright in 1979 and 1980. Because there is no postseason for Ivy League champions, there's no reason to break ties at the top of the league. As a result, there have been twenty-five seasons in fifty-seven years in which two or three teams have shared Ivy League title.

"We were all very aware of the fact that Yale hadn't gone back-to-back in more than forty years," team captain Wande Owens said. "We wanted team 150 to be the team that ended the streak."

Perhaps because Ivy League schools have been playing football for so long, season numbers are tracked very carefully. Yale's helmets all had a "150" on the back, and no one referred to the "150th season for Yale football." It was simply "Team 150." Harvard was also playing for the 150th season. Princeton, which played in the first college football game against Rutgers in 1869 (the final score was 6–4) wears "1869" on its helmets.

"I feel like we were running in the mud the first part of the season," Reno said. "We had a team meeting the day after the Penn game and talked about that it was time to just play, to not worry about how the end of the season was going to feel but how the next play was going to feel. That's a coaching cliché, but it's an important one."

Whether it was the semi-come-to-Jesus meeting, the good weather (at last), or just finally playing to their potential, Yale was in control of Columbia right from the beginning and didn't let up until the fourth quarter.

Fabish opened the game with a new quarterback, hoping to spark his offense. Caden Bell went to the bench, replaced in the lineup by fellow senior Joe Green. This was a tough decision for Fabish because Bell was a captain and a clear-cut leader in the locker room.

But his struggles to throw the ball downfield and the fact that the Lions had scored 26 points in three conference games left Fabish searching for a way to get enough points from his offense to give the defense a chance to win games.

The defense ranked number one in scoring in the FCS and yet the Lions were 0–3 in the Ivy League coming into the game. Their two victories had been against Georgetown and Marist—both shutouts. They had also held Princeton's offense to 10 points and produced the team's only points on a pick-six touchdown, losing 10–7.

Yale, however, dominated the Columbia defense largely because Grooms finally looked like the 2022 Ivy League Player of the Year that he had been. The Bulldogs put together three long touchdown drives—70 yards in ten plays, 75 yards in thirteen, and 85 in thirteen in the first half. Meanwhile, the quarterback change didn't get anything done for Columbia's offense and it was 21–0 at halftime.

The third quarter was scoreless, but Yale began the fourth quarter by stopping Columbia on a fourth down at the Yale 48. Grooms then threw a swing pass to Mason Tipton, who took the ball all the way to the 13. From there, Grooms took it into the end zone to make it 28–0 with 14:21 to play, ending any Columbia hopes for a miracle comeback.

Yale added a fifth touchdown before the Lions finally broke the shutout with a 74-yard drive that culminated on a 17-yard Green-to-Jack-Larsen pass with eleven seconds left.

The 35–7 final was the first time all season that Columbia had lost by a one-sided score and the first time the Lions had given up more than twenty points. It was also the first time that Yale had looked like the team that was trying to win a second straight championship.

"I think we realized after the Penn game that we were out of excuses and out of time," Grooms said. "One more loss and we were done in the conference race. We finally started to play like the team we knew we could be."

The win put everyone in the Yale locker room in a good mood although no one was celebrating. One win when four were needed was hardly reason to throw a party.

Not surprisingly, the mood across the field was much darker. Not only had the Lions suffered their worst loss of the season, but they had also lost Mason Tomlin for the rest of the season. Tomlin was one of two football-playing sons of Pittsburgh Steelers coach Mike Tomlin. His older brother Dino was a wide receiver at Boston College. He had transferred there after two seasons at Maryland and had become a productive player who would finish his senior season with twenty-four catches, including five in a win over Syracuse.

Mason was small for a defensive back—small for any position on a college football field—at five feet eight and 155 pounds. But he loved football. His speed made him an asset to any team. He had played wide receiver, running back, and safety in high school and was recruited by a number of FCS schools because of his speed and his excellent grades.

He finally decided on Columbia over William and Mary—alma mater of both his parents—because he liked the idea of going to an Ivy League school and being in New York. He saw his postgraduation future in music—both performing and in production—and figured New York would be a good place to be during his college years.

Tomlin actually looks more like a musician than a football player. He wears thick glasses off the field and his hair is cut in dreadlocks. He has an infectious smile and laugh. It is easy to picture him performing in a New York coffee shop and charming audiences.

He played as a nickel back and on special teams for three seasons. There was no football during his freshman year. At Yale, he started at safety and got tangled up with a blocker on the first series of the game.

"It was just a weird kind of hit," he said. "I went down and I felt tingling in both my arms and a little bit dizzy. No way was I coming out. I just kept playing through it although the pain was getting worse.

"By the second half, I really couldn't play. I was whiffing on tackles, missing plays I should have made easily. I had a feeling I was concussed but I didn't tell anybody."

Remarkably, Tomlin made five tackles in what would be his last college football game. When he missed what should have been an easy tackle, Fabish subbed for him. "Actually that's when I knew

I was really out of it," he said. "I started yelling at him, really yelling. If there's one thing I learned growing up as my father's son, it's that you *never* yell at your coach. I just melted down. I knew I was really hurt and there was nothing I could do about it. I lost it. That's when they took me to the blue (injury) tent.

"I told them about the stingers in my arms and that I'd had them all game. They took me right to the hospital from there. They x-rayed me and then gave me an MRI. I was concussed—third time in my career. I pretty much knew that was it. First person I called was my dad. He said, 'You've had a really good run. Try not to be too upset.'

"Actually, I was okay. I hated the idea that I was through playing football, but I realized how lucky I was to get to play for as long as I played. Football is a rough game, but I loved every second I got to play. I just wish we'd won a few more games my last season. We had winning seasons when I was a sophomore and a junior. But things didn't fall our way my senior year. That's football—that's sports. You give everything you have and sometimes it's just not quite enough."

# Chapter Ten

THE SEVENTH WEEK OF THE Ivy League season began on Friday night when Brown played at Penn.

Before the game, the two schools held a reception to commemorate the fiftieth anniversary of the first Division I game in which two Black quarterbacks opposed one another. Martin Vaughn had been Penn's quarterback and Dennis Coleman quarterbacked Brown that long-ago afternoon. Both were from Pennsylvania and both had been recruited by Division I-A (FBS) schools before landing in the Ivy League for various reasons—ranging from their size to the color of their skin.

In a piece published ten days after the 2023 game, NCAA.com's Maya Ellison pointed out that "the term [Black quarterback] was something of a foreign language in those days."

Penn won that 1973 game, 28–20, and Coleman and Vaughn became lifelong friends. The Ivy League's unofficial mayor, Jack Ford, emceed the ceremony, and the two men took part in the toss of the coin on an unseasonably warm evening (70 degrees, almost no wind at kickoff) with 4,735 in attendance. Rush-hour traffic on a Friday night in Philadelphia was always bound to affect attendance. But, what TV wanted, TV got. The fact that people could stay home and watch on over-the-air TV also had an effect on attendance.

The game proved to be worth fighting the traffic for those who made it to Franklin Field. Both quarterbacks, Penn's Aidan Sayin and Brown's Jake Willcox, had big nights throwing the ball. Willcox completed twenty-six of thirty-seven passes for 250 yards and rushed for another 40—and Sayin threw for 322 yards on thirty-two of fifty-five. The difference was that, with his team behind most of the second half, Sayin was forced to throw the ball on almost every play and he was intercepted three times.

The last of those interceptions came with exactly one minute left. Sayin had thrown a 12-yard touchdown pass to Jared Richardson with more than eight minutes left to close Brown's lead to 30–24. The Penn defense forced a punt and the Quakers took over with plenty of time left—4:21—at their own 22. They drove the ball to the Brown 8. But on third-and-eight, Sayin's pass in the end zone to Jared Richardson (who had twelve catches for 112 yards) was intercepted by Isaiah Reed.

After Brown took a safety, Penn got one more possession but could only get as far as the Brown 49 before Sayin was sacked looking to throw a Hail Mary on the last play of the game.

"That was a tough one to take," said Joey Slackman, who was involved in eleven tackles. "We knew they were good coming in, especially the quarterback [Willcox]. It just seemed as if whenever they really needed a play, he made a play. We knew what was at stake in terms of winning the league and, in the end, we just couldn't get it done.

"Gave us two losses—one in overtime in the league and one in which we could have won the game in the last minute. Frustrating."

Brown's victory left both teams at 2–2. They were tied with Dartmouth, Yale, and Cornell, and all five teams were one game behind Harvard and Princeton at 3–1. The Tigers had gone to Cornell and almost pitched a shutout, beating the Big Red, 14–3. Harvard had bounced back from its loss at Princeton to beat Dartmouth 20–9 at Harvard Stadium. Only Columbia, still winless, wasn't within a game of the lead.

"When I first came into the league in 2019, I thought there was a lot of parity then," Dartmouth quarterback Nick Howard said. "But last season, I think there was even more parity. Columbia finished last, but their defense was really good. It seemed like every week when we read our scouting report, it said something about the defense being one of the top-ranked in the country. Every week we were facing a good defense. It was the kind of challenge you really enjoy if you're a competitor."

The best news for Dartmouth had come on October 18—while they were preparing to play Columbia. They had been called into their meeting room and informed by athletic director Mike Harrity that Sammy McCorkle's interim tag was being removed and he was now their head coach.

"Put it this way, if they had done anything else, I think we would all have been really upset," Howard said. "Coach Mac had done such a great job making sure we kept things together, that we kept pushing forward no matter what happened on and off the field. We thought it should happen and that it would happen, but we were still nervous because we didn't *know* what was going to happen. It was a relief and it was great for all of us to hear."

The room had exploded with cheers when Harrity made the announcement. He was a new athletic director, having been named in June of 2022. Often, a new athletic director will want his own person for the two most important jobs on campus—football coach and men's basketball coach.

Clearly, Teevens had been untouchable; he was part of Dartmouth's fabric. McCorkle had been at the school for nineteen years but had never been a head coach. To his credit, Harrity understood the uniqueness of the tragic situation and decided not to make everyone sweat out the season. That's why he made the decision to end the suspense.

"He called me in a couple days earlier; I think it was on Monday," McCorkle remembered. "We had just lost to Colgate so I think I was a little bit nervous—you are always a little bit nervous when your boss calls you in, especially right after a loss.

"But as soon as I walked in, Mike said, 'I want to take the interim tag off your title; I'd like you to be our next coach.'

"There was a contract on his desk. He said, 'You may want to think about it for a couple days, it's up to you.' I signed it right then and there. It was an emotional moment for me."

It was an emotional moment for everyone—staff, players, everyone involved with the program—when the announcement was officially made that Thursday. The Big Green went out and beat Columbia that Saturday before losing at Harvard the following week.

"Wrong week to catch them," McCorkle said. "They were upset about losing to Princeton, and they played with that proverbial chip on their shoulder—especially their defense."

Harvard won 17–9, keeping Dartmouth out of the end zone all afternoon.

Harvard captain Nate Leskovec didn't see the win as a chip-on-the-shoulder thing as much as a looking-in-the-mirror game. "We knew we weren't good against Princeton," he said. "We got behind and came back, but we couldn't keep them from scoring with the game on the line. That wasn't acceptable. We had to be better against Dartmouth and, fortunately, we were."

McCorkle and several of his coaches talked on the two-hour bus ride home about where their season was at that moment. They were 4–3 overall and 2–2 in the conference, the losses being to Yale and Harvard.

"The question was, where was our season going?" McCorkle said. "We'd played respectably in the losses to Yale and Harvard, had a chance to win both games—especially the one at Yale. But playing respectably wasn't the goal. We had three games left that we could win or we could lose—Princeton, Cornell, and Brown.

"We could still win the league—heck, at that moment everyone other than Columbia had a chance to win the league. I wanted the players to be thinking in terms of trying to win the league. That meant we had to sweep."

When the team met the next day, that was McCorkle's message. The time for coming close was past. There was no more margin for error. "It wasn't quite a come-to-Jesus meeting," McCorkle said. "But it was close.

"When Mike told me he was giving me the job, I wanted to be sure he was doing the right thing not just for this season, but for the future, for the short term and the long term. Now, the short term was right in front of us. It was all there for us if we went out and took it."

At that moment, that was true of seven teams. There were three weeks left to go.

---

The last Friday night game of the season was the following week at Dartmouth, with Princeton coming to town.

In a sense, it was an elimination game for both teams. Princeton had some cushion at 3–1 and was tied for first with Harvard. Dartmouth had no cushion. It was one of the five 2–2 teams, meaning it was—literally—an elimination game for the Big Green. A third loss would eliminate them from any chance to win or tie for the title. No team in Ivy League history had won or tied for the championship with three losses.

In fact, two-loss teams had tied for the title only twice—Dartmouth and Princeton in 1963; and Dartmouth, Harvard, and Princeton in 1982.

A night game in November at Dartmouth can be risky because snow is certainly possible and cold weather is a virtual certainty. For this game, the teams got lucky. The temperature was in the thirties at kickoff, but there wasn't much wind and no sign of precipitation.

"If you have to play up there in November, that's about as good as you can hope for," Princeton coach Bob Surace said.

Beyond the weather, the best news for Princeton was that Jalen Travis was back in the lineup with a game [at Cornell] under his belt and his MCL finally feeling healthy.

"It was torture sitting out, especially the Harvard game," Travis said. "One thing about the Ivy League is that any game you miss is a big deal because there are only ten of them. Not being able to play against Harvard really hurt." He smiled. "Winning helped a lot."

Princeton came into the game 3–1 in the league but with a difficult remaining schedule: at Dartmouth, Yale at home, and at Penn. Additionally, every team in the league, with the exception of

Columbia, came into the final three weeks still having a mathematical chance to at least share the title.

"You want to win outright," Travis said. "But if you tie for first, you're still a champion and that feels pretty good too."

For all of Dartmouth's struggles in the previous twelve months, it had won league titles in 2019 and 2021, both times going 9–1 overall and 6–1 in conference play. Each of its losses had been at home and had been surprises. In 2019, Cornell had come onto Memorial Field and pulled a 20–17 upset, and, two years later, after the COVID nonseason in 2020, Columbia had shut the Big Green out, 19–0, on a Friday night.

Then came the disastrous 2022 season, which led to a lot of off-season meetings among players and coaches—even before Teevens's accident—about getting back to being the kind of team Dartmouth expected to be.

"We went from confident to cocky," running back Q Jones said. "In '21, we made plays when we had to. We pulled out close games because we knew the games were going to be close. If we got behind, it didn't catch us off guard. We'd just dug in and made the plays we had to make. In '22, it was just the opposite. We thought we were entitled to win close games, that it would happen because we were Dartmouth. No one is entitled to win."

Jones was a remarkable story. He'd been a star growing up in Colorado. Prior to his junior year, he had received interest from virtually the entire Pac-12 and seemed destined to play FBS football somewhere. Then, in the state championship game at the end of his sophomore year, he broke his left leg badly enough that doctors had to put a rod in it. He then rebroke the leg in the opening game of his junior year and missed the entire season.

By the time he was well enough to play as a senior, COVID had shut down high school football in Colorado. With no football, he worked part-time at Walmart when it reopened, to make some money.

"I was lost," he said. "I was banking on football to get me into college and suddenly I hadn't played for more than two years and it looked like it might be three. I had *no* offers. It was a pretty terrible time."

Then a cousin offered to put him up in Arizona so he could play football there. As he was getting ready to make the move, the Colorado High School Activities Association voted to allow a seven-game season, so he opted to remain in Colorado. The season was only seven games, but it was enough. He won the same Gold Helmet award that Christian McCaffery had won as a high school senior that goes to "the state's top football player, scholar-athlete, and citizen." Colleges began showing up again. His first offer came from the Air Force Academy, but that wasn't the direction he wanted to go in.

He had always had good grades but when he was first contacted by Dartmouth assistant coach Cheston Blackshear, he had no idea what Dartmouth was or where it was located. "I did a little homework at that point," he said. "I knew what the Ivy League was and how prestigious it was academically and I liked the idea of an Ivy League school. It was a chance to change the narrative. No one in my family had gone to college much less to an Ivy League school. The financials they offered were good. So, the decision was really kind of easy at that point."

He only got into three games as a freshman but became a starter as a sophomore and was the team's second-leading rusher. Like everyone else at Dartmouth, he knew that the Princeton game was a make-or-break game for both teams, but especially for Dartmouth.

"We lose, we're out," Jones said. "Everyone knows you don't win the Ivy League with three losses."

A small crowd of 2,526 gathered at Memorial Field for the seven o'clock kickoff. No doubt a number of fans stayed home rather than deal with the elements—even on a relatively mild New Hampshire November evening—knowing the game was on real television and not just streaming. Even so, the players enjoy playing on Friday night, knowing they are on national TV.

Most Ivy League stadiums have only added lights in recent years. Some of the lights are very good—others not so good. Dartmouth had to receive approval from the town of Hanover when it installed lights in 2011. The last Ivy League team to install lights was Yale, which brought in temporary lights for a 2:30 kickoff against Harvard in 2015.

Dartmouth's lights (like Harvard's) are less-than-great. Watching from inside the stadium isn't easy, and the field looks almost dark on TV. The field itself is well-lit, the rest of the eleven-thousand-seat stadium not so much.

Princeton was the hottest team in the Ivy League coming into the game, not just because the Tigers had won two games in a row but because of who they had beaten in those two games and how they had won the games.

They had blown a 14–0 lead against Harvard before a late touchdown had given them a 21–14 win. That victory had not only thrown the league race wide open but was special for the Princeton seniors.

"We never lost to them," said linebacker Ozzie Nicholas, one of the team's co-captains. "Let's be honest, that's a big deal. Harvard's good—they're always good—but we all feel like they think they're on some sort of pedestal. We don't look at it that way—either on the football field or off it. They have an attitude that makes beating them feel special.

"I respect them, but I certainly don't like them."

A week after the Harvard win, with a letdown entirely possible, the Tigers won 14–3 at Cornell—the defense shutting down Cornell quarterback Jameson Wang every time the Big Red got close to the goal line. Wang's numbers were good—twenty-six of forty-two passing for 234 yards—but Princeton held Cornell to a second-quarter Jackson Kennedy field goal.

In the meantime, Princeton quarterback Blake Stenstrom had arguably his best game of the year, throwing touchdown passes to Tamatoa Falatea (77 yards) and Luke Colella (33 yards) while throwing for 299 yards without an interception.

"We were really confident going into the Dartmouth game," Nicholas said. "Then we got off to a bad start and made mental errors we hadn't been making. They were good and they were on a mission. But we never should have lost that game. Never."

The bad start came on Princeton's first offensive series. Dartmouth had gone three-and-out and Princeton took over on its own 21. On the first play of the drive, Stenstrom tried to throw a pass over the middle. But it was deflected to sophomore Sean Williams, whose nickname among his teammates was "the playmaker."

Williams was a five-foot-nine safety who had started eight games as a freshman. He grabbed the deflected ball, cut to the outside, and went down the sideline for a 26-yard pick-six touchdown. The game was less than three minutes old and the Big Green led, 7–0.

They stretched the lead to 10–0. This was the first time all season that Princeton had trailed early or by more than a touchdown. In fact, the Tigers had led into the fourth quarter in their three losses—two of which had ended in overtime.

To their credit, they were undaunted by the early deficit. They pieced together two second-quarter drives, both capped by John Volker runs—one for 1 yard, the other for 9. In spite of another Princeton turnover—a fumble by Luke Colella—Dartmouth couldn't mount any offense and Princeton led, 14–10, at the break.

The teams traded third-quarter touchdowns, Dartmouth driving 57 yards to retake the lead at 17–14 before Stenstrom found a wide-open Colella down the left sideline for a 62-yard score that put Princeton back in the lead 21–17.

Owen Zalc, Dartmouth's freshman kicker, closed the gap to 21–20, and the game became a defensive struggle in the fourth quarter.

After a missed Princeton field goal with 6:04 left, Dartmouth began driving with the clock running down. McCorkle had used three quarterbacks during the evening—Nick Howard when he wanted to run the ball and Jackson Proctor and Dylan Cadwallader when he was more likely to pass. Now, with the game on the line, McCorkle alternated Howard and Proctor. On third-and-two from the Princeton 30, with the clock under two minutes, running back Tevita Moimoi went up the middle but came up a yard short of the first down.

McCorkle had a choice to make: go for it on fourth-and-one or bring in the freshman kicker Zalc for a 47-yard-field goal attempt. Zalc was a little guy—five feet ten and 155 pounds—with a big leg from Cary, North Carolina, a suburb of Raleigh, perhaps best known as the place where iconic basketball coach Jim Valvano had lived prior to this death in 1993.

Zalc had been place-kicking and punting all season for Dartmouth and had proven he could handle pressure. He had kicked the game-winning field goal in overtime at Penn, had made a 54-yarder two weeks earlier against Columbia, and had made three field goals to provide all of Dartmouth's scoring in the 17–9 loss to Harvard.

It was more than that though that led to McCorkle's decision.

"He's just got a great demeanor for a kicker," he said. "He's always calm, make or miss. He kicks the ball and is ready to move on to whatever comes next. I knew he had the leg to make a 47-yarder and I didn't think the pressure would get to him. I also had a lot of respect for Princeton's defense. I thought the right thing was to put the ball on Owen's foot."

Zalc trotted in with 1:34 left. What happened next was perhaps best described by Jack Ford. "That was right down the middle," he said watching the replay of the kick. "I mean it was going nowhere but down the middle. And watch his reaction: 'I kicked it, it's good, and that's it.' Almost no emotion. He just does his job."

There was plenty of reaction from his Dartmouth teammates: Glee and lots of hugs. Zalc even gave a couple of fist bumps.

"I almost never do that," he said. "I treated it like just another kick when Coach Mac sent me in. But when I made it, I realized it was a pretty big deal."

The game wasn't over. There was still 1:29 on the clock. A field goal could still win the game for Princeton. Stenstrom quickly completed a pass to Falatea for 16 yards to the Tigers 41. But two incomplete passes and a 4-yard Stenstrom run later, Princeton faced fourth-and-six from its own 46 with forty-one seconds left. Stenstrom tried to find Colella, his most reliable receiver, but cornerback Jordan Washington broke the pass up.

Princeton was out of time-outs. The game was over: Dartmouth 23, Princeton 21.

uddy Teevens, the heart and soul of Dartmouth. *John Risley, courtesy of Dartmouth Athletics*

im Murphy, the winningest coach in Ivy League history—two hundred wins in thirty years at
arvard. *Courtesy of Harvard Athletics*

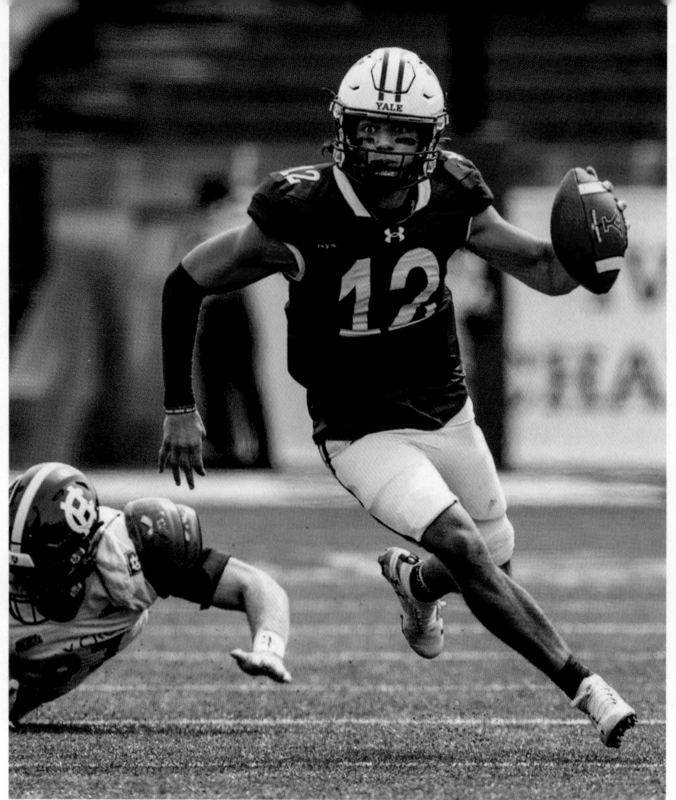


Nolan Grooms—lefty, Southerner, and a two-time Ivy Player of the Year at Yale. *Courtesy of Yale Athletics*

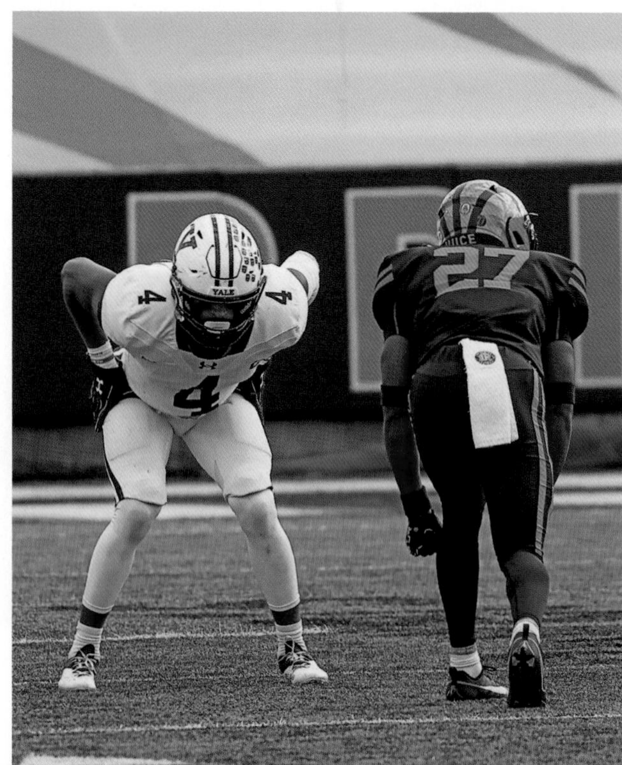


Wande Owens—Yale's 2023 captain; he has The Game's game ball. *Courtesy of Yale Athletics*

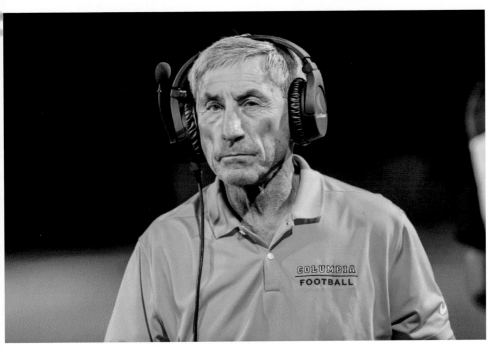

Al Bagnoli—he did the impossible at Columbia: he won games. *Courtesy of Stockton Photo/ Columbia Athletics*

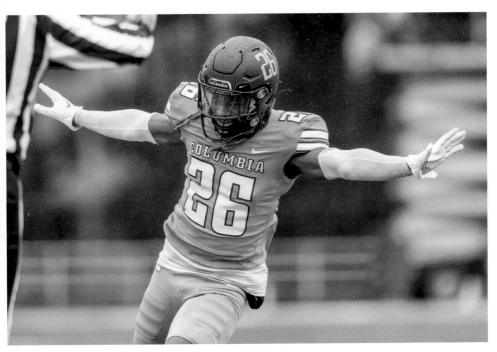

Mason Tomlin—a football coach's son with music in his future. *Courtesy of Stockton Photo/ Columbia Athletics*

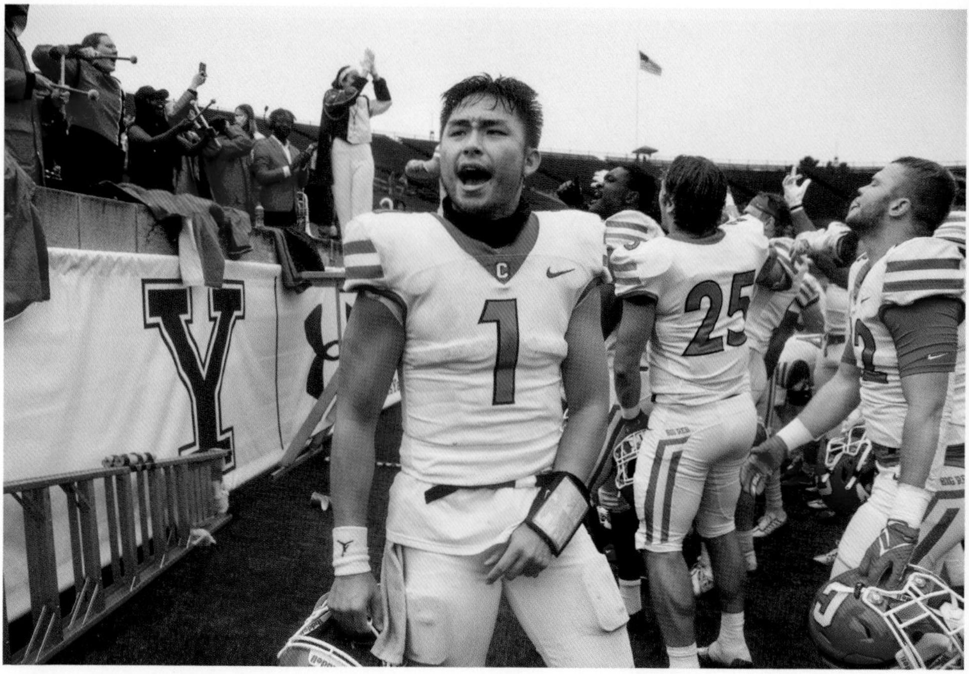

Jameson Wang—Cornell's quarterback whose strength is the chip on his shoulder. *Courtesy of Cornell Athletics*

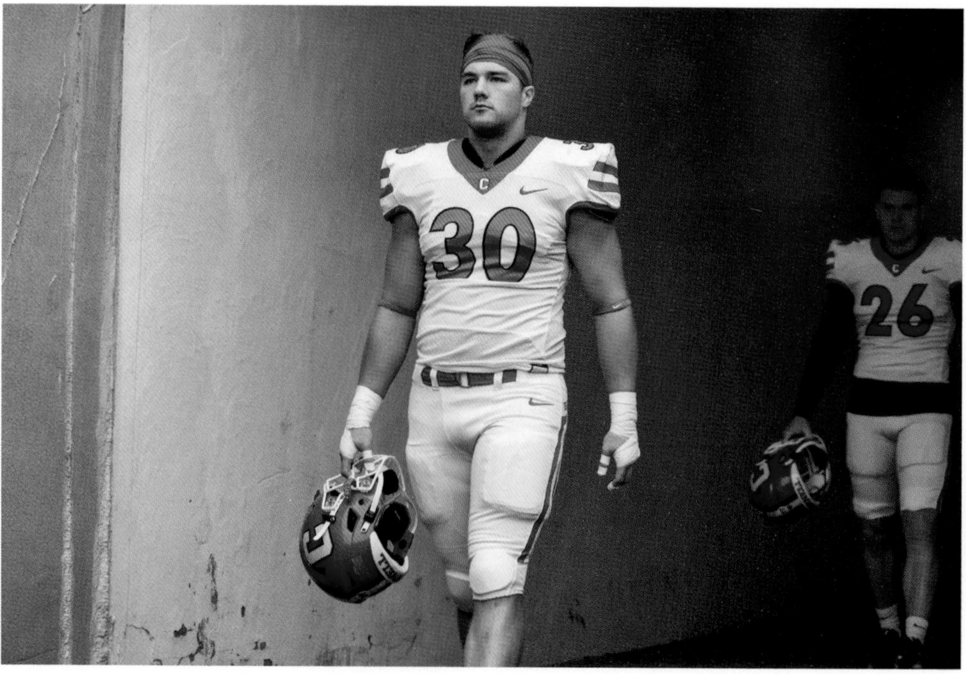

Jake Stebbins—his injury changed the arc of Cornell's season. *Courtesy of Cornell Athletics*

Ozzie Nicholas—no one in the league played with more enthusiasm. *Brain Foley, courtesy of Princeton Athletics*

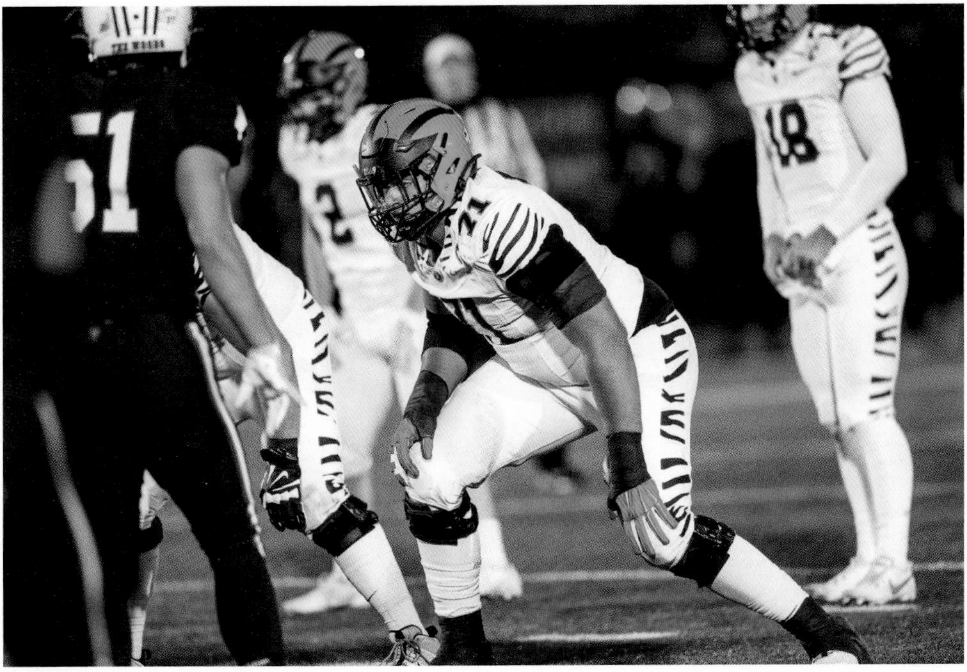

Jalen Travis—NFL scouts came to Princeton to see him. A leader on and off the football field. *Brain Foley, courtesy of Princeton Athletics*

Jake Willcox—in a league full of excellent quarterbacks, Brown's was as good as any. *Courtesy of Brown Athletics*

Wes Rockett—two catches as a Brown freshman, *seventy-one* as a senior. *Chip DeLorenzo, courtesy of Brown Athletics*

Jake Bingham—he stepped up after his roommate's death and played brilliantly for Penn. *Aaron Mitchell, courtesy of Penn Athletics*

Joey Slackman—arrived at Penn as a wrestler, left as a football Player of the Year *Aaron Mitchell, courtesy of Penn Athletics*

Nate Leskovec—Harvard's captain and quiet leader. *Courtesy of Harvard Athletics*

Sammy McCorkle—from coach *for* a year to coach *of* the year. *Suzanna Koscho, courtesy of Dartmouth Athletics*

"That was the biggest win we'd had in a while," McCorkle said. "Penn was certainly a big win, but at that stage of the season knowing what was at stake, which was to stay in the conference race, it was bigger. And the way we fell behind after leading and kept our poise was impressive.

"I knew in the spring we had a tough group after Coach T's accident. I knew it even more after that game."

The flip side was Princeton, which had been tied for first place coming in. "We had our fate in our own hands," Nicholas said. "We'd worked hard to get there. Then, we let it get away. Credit to Dartmouth, but that loss was on us."

There were three games the next day. Brown couldn't maintain its momentum after the win at Penn, losing 36–17 at home to Yale—which, all of a sudden, was looking like Yale. Cornell and Columbia continued to slide: the Big Red traveled to Philadelphia and were soundly beaten, 23–8, by Penn, and Columbia's defense struggled for a second straight week, losing handily, 38–24, in New York to Harvard.

Harvard's win, combined with Princeton's loss, put the Crimson back alone in first place at 4–1. Princeton, Yale, Dartmouth, and Penn were all a game back at 3–2; Brown and Cornell were both 2–3, and Columbia remained winless in league play at 0–5.

While neither Cornell nor Columbia had any chance at the league title, both Dave Archer and Mark Fabish understood that their jobs were probably on the line the last two weeks.

"It was my tenth season," Archer said. "We'd been close, but after ten years, close wasn't enough. I think I always felt, especially after we'd gone 5–5 and had an All-Ivy quarterback returning, that this was likely to be an up-or-out season. I understood that."

It wasn't going to get easier for Cornell, having to travel to Dartmouth—never an easy trip, especially in November, but even more so when the Big Green still had a chance to at least tie for the conference title.

"After the Princeton game, we still believed we had a legitimate chance to tie for the title," quarterback Nick Howard said. "We beat a very good team that night. We saw no reason not to win those last two games. We still needed someone to beat Harvard, but we believed that was possible since they had to beat two good teams [Penn and Yale]."

Columbia had a home game left against Brown and then had to travel to Cornell for a game that might decide the fate of both coaches.

In the season's penultimate week, Yale would travel to Princeton and Harvard would host Penn. All four teams still had a chance to at least share the title. Yale-Princeton was an elimination game. The same was true for Penn. Harvard, on the other hand, had a chance to at least clinch a share of the title with one game to play.

Tim Murphy was trying to win his two hundredth game as Harvard's coach and, more importantly, clinch a tenth Ivy League title in his thirty years as the Crimson's coach.

It had been a difficult and emotional season for Murphy in the wake of Buddy Teevens's death.

"I think about him every day," he said that week. "How can I not? You know someone for fifty-five years and then they're gone, it has to shake you up. Standing on the sideline when we played Dartmouth, I didn't dare look across the field. I always tried not to look across the field when I coached against Buddy for seventeen years, but it was harder to think about looking over there when he *wasn't* there."

Like Dartmouth and Teevens, Murphy and Harvard had been looking for a bounce back year. Both had struggled in 2022—Dartmouth dropping to 3–7 after back-to-back 9–1 seasons and

Harvard going 6–4 and finishing fourth in the league, a rare low for the Crimson.

Dartmouth had been to hell and back during the offseason, but so had Murphy because of Teevens's accident and subsequent death.

"He had talked to us about it," Harvard team captain Nate Leskovec. "You could tell how much it affected him whenever he brought it up, especially after Coach Teevens died. My heart went out to him but also to all the Dartmouth players. I'd gotten to know some of them during my time at Harvard and they were a very classy group."

In a strict football sense, both teams had quarterback questions. All three of Harvard's quarterbacks from 2022 had graduated and the Crimson entered summer practice not sure who the starter would be.

Dartmouth coach Sammy McCorkle never had a firm grip on who he wanted behind center: Nick Howard was easily the best runner of the group and Jackson Proctor and Dylan Cadwallader were both good passers. All three played at times, and all three had ups and downs—but more ups as the season wore on.

Charles DePrima won the starting job for Harvard and was probably the Player of the Year the first half of the season. But, as Ozzie Nicholas pointed out, Princeton's defense found a way to shut him down and he appeared to lose confidence after that. Two weeks later, Murphy decided to go with sophomore Jaden Craig at quarterback and he remained the starter for the rest of the season.

"I know how tough a decision that was for the coaches," Leskovec said. "It was tough on us too. Charles had been *so* good the first half of the season and we just thought of him as our quarterback. Jaden is an amazing talent. He can run and he has a cannon for an arm. Charles had struggled a little but it was tough not seeing him on the field."

Remarkably, three of the four games played on the second Saturday in November went to overtime. At Princeton, the Tigers and Yale swung back and forth all afternoon—each team making plays when it seemed as if the other was about to take control of the game.

Princeton had been 8–0 the previous season and seemingly in control of the league race when it went to Yale and lost, 24–20. Princeton had led 14–7 at halftime before Yale outscored it 17–0 in the third quarter and hung on to win. A week later, Penn had beaten Princeton 20–19, scoring the winning touchdown on the game's last play on a fourth-down play from the 5 yard line. Everyone from Princeton was convinced the play clock had hit zero before the last snap.

"It had run out," Bob Surace said. "At the very least, they should have had fourth down from the 10, not the 5."

A year later, both teams knew that whoever won the game would go into the season's last week with a chance to at least tie for the title.

Yale came out flying, driving 75 yards on thirteen plays with Nolan Grooms capping the drive with a 25-yard run to take a quick 7–0 lead. But an excellent Brady Clark punt pinned Yale at the 7 yard line and, after the Tigers forced a three-and-out, they got the ball back on the Yale 30 after a short Jack Bosman punt. From there, it took Princeton seven plays to get into the end zone, John Volker punching it in from the five to tie the score at 7–7.

That was the halftime score. The teams traded third-quarter touchdowns and it stayed 14–14 until Yale went back in front midway through the fourth quarter. But, in a game where neither team could seem to convert on anything deep, Princeton did quite suddenly.

On the first play after the kickoff, Stenstrom found Luke Colella wide open down the left sideline. Yale had missed a coverage and Colella was 10 yards behind the defense. That made the score 21–21.

All of a sudden, the defensive struggle became a shootout. Yale marched 70 yards to a go-ahead score, the drive climaxed by a 21-yard run by Joshua Pitsenberger with 7:10 left in the game.

Patiently, Princeton came right back. Just as it had done in the Columbia game, the Tigers made big plays when it appeared all might be lost. First, Stenstrom found Colella for 11 yards on a fourth-and-five from the Yale 35. Then, after Stenstrom had been sacked for a 9-yard loss to set up fourth-and-eighteen at the 32, he scrambled desperately and somehow found Tamatoa Falatea, 1 yard beyond the first down marker at the 13.

"In that situation you have to be aware of where the marker is," Stenstrom said. "But once the play starts, you have to rely on instinct. Tamatoa did a great job finding the open spot just where he needed to be."

Four plays later, Princeton faced yet *another* fourth down—this time at the 1, just as in the Columbia game, with the clock running down. Surace went for a change of pace, bringing backup quarterback Blaine Hipa into the game. Hipa was more of a runner than Stenstrom. Yale looked for a quarterback sneak or a dive into the line.

Hipa faked the run, then popped up and found Colella open in the end zone for a touchdown that tied the game with 16 seconds left.

Overtime—with two seasons on the line.

Neither team scored in the first overtime: Princeton went for it on fourth down from the 2 but finally ran out of fourth-down magic when Yale captain Wande Owens broke up Stenstrom's pass to Colella in the end zone. The Tigers then forced the Bulldogs into a

35-yard field goal attempt and Jack Bosman missed it, wide left by about two feet.

Yale got the ball first in the second overtime and didn't take long to score: A Grooms pass to CJ Thompson from the 25 yard line picked up 12; a Grooms run got the ball to the 3. From there, Pitsenberger slammed it in for his third touchdown of the game. Yale converted the mandatory two-point conversion and it was 36–28.

Needing to score and convert the two-point conversion to keep the game alive, Princeton came up 12 yards short with Stenstrom's fourth-down pass broken up—again—by Wande Owens.

Yale walked off the field knowing it still had a chance to win the league title. Princeton walked off heartbroken.

"All I've ever asked of any team I've played on was to leave everything on the field," Jalen Travis said. "It's a cliché, but it's true. We gave everything we had that day. They were just a little bit better than we were. It hurt, it will always hurt, but I know we all gave everything we possibly could."

Princeton was now 4–5 overall—two of the losses in overtime and the other three decided late in the fourth quarter.

"That's the thing about the Ivy League," Surace said. "At the end of the season, the teams that finish on top have at least a couple of games they easily could have lost. And teams like ours in 2022 and 2023 were a play or two from being on top. In 2022, we were a couple plays from being undefeated. Believe it or not, we were pretty close in 2023 too.

"We just have to try to come back next year and turn those plays around."

Princeton would open the 2024 season at Lehigh on September 21. It would be a long wait.

---

The only team that had its fate completely in its own hands going into week nine was Harvard. The Crimson had bounced back from their loss to Princeton by beating Dartmouth and then by traveling to New York to beat Columbia.

Jaden Craig had taken over as Harvard's quarterback a week after the Princeton game when Charles DePrima had been intercepted twice in the first half against Dartmouth. Craig's numbers weren't spectacular in the second half, but he led Harvard on an eleven-play, 75-yard drive, culminated by his 3-yard run to make the final score 17–9.

Murphy decided to stick with Craig the next week, and the Crimson offense had put up 38 points against a good Columbia defense.

A win over Penn would clinch at least a share of the Ivy League title. As much success as Murphy had enjoyed, Harvard hadn't won an Ivy League title since 2015, when it had tied with Dartmouth and Penn, all with 6–1 league records.

Winning the title in any form would mean a lot to Murphy and to his players, all of whom knew what a difficult season it had been for him and who suspected he might step down at season's end.

"We didn't want to think in those terms," 2024 captain Shane McLaughlin said. "But we also knew how close he and Coach Teevens were and that it had to be on his mind."

Even though he hadn't made a decision, the thought of retirement was certainly on Murphy's mind, especially running onto the field at Harvard Stadium for what he knew might be his last home game.

Penn jumped to a quick 10–0 lead before Harvard turned the game around in the second quarter and took a 20–10 lead at halftime. Penn wasn't done. The Quakers' defense shut Harvard out in the second half and tied the game at 20–20 on a 69-yard drive, bridging the third and fourth quarters with running back Malachi Mosley diving in from the 1 with 11:04 left in the game.

Neither team could score for the rest of regulation, each missing a late field goal attempt.

On they went to overtime.

They traded successful field goals in the first overtime. After Albert Jang converted from 36 yards to give Penn a 23–20 lead, Harvard drove to the Penn 2 yard line with a first down. But the Quakers' defense dug in, giving up just 1 yard on the next three plays. The most dramatic of those plays came on second down when Joey Slackman, who had been told by the Penn doctors on the sideline that his career was over just a few plays earlier after he broke his collarbone, stepped into the hole and somehow brought Shane McLaughlin down short of the goal line.

"I knew I was done and I wasn't going to be able to play the next week," Slackman said. "The doctors said I would need surgery. I figured if I was going to need surgery anyway, I'd go out on my terms, not the doctors'. So, I told coach he better not even think about trying to stop me from going back in. It hurt like hell to make that tackle, but I'm very glad I got the chance to make it."

On fourth down, Tim Murphy took the conservative approach and sent Cali Canaval in for the chip-shot field goal that tied the game, this time at 23–23.

On to the second overtime. Harvard had the ball first and absolutely nothing went right. A holding penalty pushed the ball back to the 35 and then Jaden Craig, forced out of the pocket, was intercepted by Logan Nash.

Now, Penn only needed a field goal to win the game. The Quakers played it close to the vest and, after picking up 6 yards on three plays, Graham Gotlieb trotted on to kick from 36 yards out. Gotlieb, who would made honorable mention All-Ivy after making fifteen of eighteen field goals on the season, was about as reliable as they came. Except, this time, he missed, the kick sailing just barely wide left.

On to overtime number three.

The NCAA has changed the overtime rules repeatedly since ties were abolished beginning in the 1996 season.

Now, if a team scores a touchdown in the second overtime, it is required to go for a two-point conversion—as Yale had done against Princeton earlier that day.

If the score is still tied after two overtimes, the ball is placed on the 3 yard line and each team attempts a two-point conversion. The first one to score without the other one matching it, wins the game.

Penn was up first, but Aidan Sayin's pass was knocked down in the end zone. Harvard could now win the game by converting its attempt. At that moment, offensive coordinator Mickey Fein suggested running a play the Crimson had never run before, pointing out to Murphy that if the play didn't work, the game would just go to a fourth overtime.

"Crimson Special," Murphy said with a grin. "I liked the idea, especially since it wasn't do-or-die. It was either do or keep playing."

The actual name of the play was the "Philly Special," which had been run successfully and quite famously by the Philadelphia Eagles in Super Bowl LII in Minneapolis. Harvard had practiced it, but never run it in a game. Murphy figured with an Ivy League title on the line, this was as good a time as any to run it.

"If nothing else, we'd have the element of surprise," he said, laughing.

The next day, several media outlets called it the "Cambridge Special," which was inaccurate since Harvard Stadium is in Boston.

Quarterback Jaden Craig took the shotgun snap (virtually every Ivy League play is run out of the shotgun) and handed off to wide receiver Scott Woods II, who was running left on what looked like a jet sweep. But Woods pitched the ball back to fellow receiver Cooper Barkate—Craig's roommate—who was running from left to right. Barkate pulled up and threw a perfect pass to Craig, who had sneaked into the end zone after handing the ball to Woods and was wide open. He caught the ball and threw his arms up in the air.

And then the celebration began.

Craig took off his helmet and started sprinting through the end zone trying to escape his on-rushing teammates.

"As soon as I saw him catch it, I knew we were going to pile on top of him," said Logan Bednar. "I wanted to be the first one to get to him, but I had no chance. He just kept running and he's a lot faster than me.

"After we all jumped on each other, I just took a minute to enjoy it all and be thankful. There were times I wasn't sure I'd get to play much with injuries and stuff that happens in college football. Then I became a starter and *finally* won a championship my senior year. Corny or not, it was a dream come true."

For most of the Harvard players, especially the seniors, it was a dream come true. None had been a part of an Ivy League championship team since the Crimson hadn't won or shared a title since 2015.

In the nine seasons from 2007 through 2015, Harvard had finished first (six times) or second. In the ensuing six seasons (no season in 2020), the Crimson hadn't finished higher than third.

"The league got better," Murphy said. "And we didn't. We had to get better to get back to the top of the league."

Even though Dartmouth and Yale could still tie them for the title in the season's final week, Harvard celebrated the championship, accepting a trophy that wasn't the actual trophy it would eventually receive. Whenever a team is in position to win or share a title, it has a copy of the championship trophy that is kept in storage for such an occasion. After the season ends, the league sends an actual trophy for its display case.

It took a while to get everyone into the locker room after all the celebrating and posing for pictures with the trophy and photos with family and friends and football alums. By the time everyone was in place and ready, Murphy was exhausted and drained. But his "Leap" was perfect.

Absolutely perfect.

# Chapter Eleven

THERE WAS NOW—SUDDENLY—ONE WEEK LEFT in the season. Harvard was alone in first place with a 5–1 record, having clinched Tim Murphy's tenth Ivy League title. Yale and Dartmouth were tied for second at 4–2. Yale had now won three in a row since Tony Reno had said it was capable of winning or losing its last four games. Dartmouth had won two straight—its last loss at Harvard.

Yale could clinch a tie for first with the Crimson by beating them in the Yale Bowl in the 139th version of The Game—which dated to 1875. The Game wasn't played six times—in 1894 and 1895 after the 1893 game became so violent that the schools agreed not to play those two years and twice during World War I and twice during World War II.

The most famous game—among many—took place in 1968 when Harvard scored 16 points in the last forty-two seconds to turn a 29–13 Yale lead into a 29–29 tie, bringing about the iconic *Harvard Crimson* headline: "Harvard Beats Yale, 29–29."

A Harvard victory would make the Crimson the 2023 outright league champion. A Yale victory would not only allow it to tie for the title but also would give Dartmouth a chance to tie for first if it could win at Brown.

Princeton, Penn, and Brown were all 3–3. Cornell was 2–5 and Columbia, after losing to Brown in overtime the previous week, was 0–6. Before the Lions left to travel to Cornell, Mark Fabish met with athletic director Peter Pilling who told him Columbia was going to begin a national search for a new coach the following week. Technically, Fabish would be part of the search, but he knew Pilling was telling him he wouldn't be the coach in 2024.

Fabish had sensed that he was in trouble prior to the Brown game and had sent an email to Pilling outlining the reasons he and his staff should be retained for 2024, which would have meant removing the "interim" tag from his title.

"I pointed to Coach Bagnoli's first couple of seasons and to Bob Surace's first couple of seasons at Princeton," he said. "Ivy League jobs aren't easy. It often takes time to get where you want to go. I had been an assistant coach until August 4th, then, boom, I was the head coach.

"I felt like we'd accomplished part of our goal—getting the kids to buy in and play hard every week. What we didn't accomplish was winning more games and that's always the bottom line."

Pilling responded to Fabish's note by asking that the two men meet the following Monday. The meeting didn't take very long. Pilling told Fabish that he planned to conduct a search beginning the following week.

"I think, looking back, Peter wanted to go outside the whole season," Fabish said. "I feel like we were fighting a windmill. I understand. In the end, coaching is about winning. It would have hurt more if we'd had a winning record, but we didn't. I wanted to be sure we didn't go into Cornell feeling defeated. We still had one more chance to win a game and I wanted the kids to feel like that was important."

The feeling at Cornell wasn't all that different. The Big Red had regressed after their fast start. They had gone into the season's seventh week 2–1 in the league—the wins over Yale and Brown—and 3–3 overall. And then the roof had fallen in. They had lost to Princeton, Penn, and Dartmouth, all by double digits, and pride was about all that was left to play for going into the Columbia game.

The importance of losing their captain and leader Jake Stebbins in the second week of the season during the victory over Yale could not be understated. Stebbins was a two-time All-Ivy linebacker who had been the defensive captain in 2022. He had decided to come back for a COVID–fifth year although he had to drop out of school in the spring of 2023 to do so. The Ivy League only allowed fifth-year players if they were still undergraduates.

"As soon as we played our last game [in 2022], I knew before we left the locker room that I wanted to play another year with these guys," Stebbins said. "I didn't want my career to end that way [with a loss at Columbia]. I love it at Cornell and, since I knew I had the chance to play, I knew right away I wanted to come back."

Not surprisingly, he was again elected captain for 2023 and almost every player on the team would tell you that they followed his lead on and off the field.

It was probably not coincidence that Cornell had started 2–0 before Stebbins tore his ACL in the Yale game. The Big Red had won once since Stebbins's injury.

"You talk about injuries, you're just making excuses," Dave Archer said. "But there are injuries and there are injuries. Losing Jake hurt us on the field the way an injury to a key starter always hurts. But he was so much the emotional leader for us that losing him meant a lot more than that."

Stebbins was a typical western Pennsylvania football player: intense and as tough as could be on the field, bright and charming off the field. Like a lot of his teammates, he was convinced that the 5–5 record in 2022 was merely a stop on the way to the top of the Ivy League. Beating Yale—at Yale—had been evidence that was possible.

"We haven't won an Ivy League title here since 1991," Stebbins said before the season started. "We all believe this is the time to change that."

If Stebbins hadn't been hurt, there is no telling what the Big Red might have done. But he did get hurt and Cornell simply wasn't the same team without him—on or off the field.

"We don't make excuses around here because that's what they are: excuses," said quarterback Jameson Wang. "We were better last year, and we honestly believed at the start of the season that this was our year. We showed it early, especially in the Yale game. But losing Jake and the injuries we had on the offensive line changed things. We hung in and we competed, but there was no margin for error. In this league, there never is."

The Big Red appeared to be in good position after it routed Brown in Ithaca in week six of the season. The victory put them at 3–3 overall but, far more important, 2–1 tied with Harvard, Penn, Dartmouth, and Princeton in the convoluted league standings.

And then, the wheels fell off—completely.

"I like to say that Ivy League football is cutthroat with class," Archer said. "Little things can kill you: injuries at the wrong position; a mental mistake at a key moment; not being able to prepare properly—we had defensive linemen practicing on offense late in the season because we'd lost nine of the eighteen offensive linemen we'd had at the start of the season.

"Or, maybe I just didn't coach well enough. As a coach, if your team doesn't live up to your expectations, you certainly have to consider that."

Regardless of the reason, Cornell lost its last four games: to Princeton, Penn, Dartmouth, and Columbia. None of the games were especially close, although the defense played well in the 14–3 loss to Princeton. After the loss to Penn in Philadelphia, Archer had a meeting with athletic director Nicki Moore.

"She told me she felt like firing me would be a step back for Cornell," Archer said. "I really think she meant it. But saying she wanted to keep me was a lot different from saying she was *going* to keep me. I think there was pressure from people outside the program who said they'd be willing to contribute more financially if a change was made. Money is always an issue at Cornell.

"Then I met with her again before we played Columbia. She said she had decided to make a change. I asked her, 'What changed?' She didn't really answer, just offered me a job as an assistant athletic director.

"I've been a coach my entire adult life, almost all of it at Cornell. I can honestly say I gave it everything I had and my coaches and players did too. But we just didn't win enough. I get that. I was in the last season of my contract, and I felt all season like it was win and get offered a new deal or lose and get shown the door."

Archer never stopped being a Cornell alum and lover of the school. When he went back to tell Moore that he wasn't going to take the job in administration, he said, "I want you to know that nothing will change my feelings about Cornell." He then handed her a check for $500.

"I want to be the first guy to show support for the new coach—regardless of who it is," he said.

Then, he left to go and prepare to coach his last game at the school.

The only one of the three remaining games that would not play a role in deciding the top of the league standings was Princeton at Penn.

Both were 3–3 in the Ivy League and both had been knocked out of the race by overtime losses the previous week. Princeton had lost 36–28 to Yale when the Bulldogs scored and converted the two-point conversion in the second overtime.

Penn had lost in three overtimes to Harvard, the game dramatically ending on the "Crimson Special" two-point conversion. It was the second overtime loss in league play for the Quakers—the first to Dartmouth. Their third loss had been 30–26 to Brown when the Bears had shut down a last-second drive inside the 10 yard line.

"That's what made it so tough emotionally," Joey Slackman said. "It wasn't as if we weren't good enough, we were. Literally one play in each game and it turns out differently. We could easily have been 6–0 going into the Princeton game. Instead, we were 3–3 and playing for pride. That wasn't the ending we had hoped for or planned."

Princeton's season hadn't been all that different. They'd certainly had success: beating Columbia on a twenty-play drive in the fourth quarter and then beating Harvard on a late touchdown. They had played three overtime games—losing to Bryant in nonleague play; blowing a 21–7 lead at Brown and losing 27–26 on a blocked extra point; and, finally, most painfully, the loss to Yale.

The real season-killer though had been the Friday night loss to Dartmouth in week eight. The Tigers had led in the fourth quarter before Owen Zalc's 47-yard field goal with 1:29 left had given the Big Green the victory. That game was a season-turner for both teams—Dartmouth in the right direction, Princeton in the wrong direction.

"Generally speaking, you remember every game you play, win or lose," said Ozzie Nicholas. "But that was one I think we'll all remember for a long time. It was a game we easily could have won. Except we didn't. That's not something you forget. We haven't won a title since 2018. That should have ended, and I think it would have if we'd beaten Dartmouth that night."

And so, Princeton and Penn couldn't finish higher than third with a win. Princeton may have had a little more to play for because Penn had beaten the Tigers at Princeton in the finale a year earlier. Even though everyone at Princeton was convinced that the Quakers hadn't gotten the last play of the game off prior to the play clock hitting zero, the play had counted, and Penn had won the game, 20–19.

That dropped Princeton to 5–2 in league play and Yale had won the title by finishing 6–1, including a win over Princeton a week earlier.

"Even though we couldn't win the championship, the game was still a big deal to us," Jalen Travis said. "They kept us from sharing the championship last year. At the very least, we wanted to go out with a win and especially with a win against *them*. If we'd been playing for *last* place, the game would have been a big deal to us—especially the seniors. We'd had so many ups and downs during the season, we didn't want our last memory of playing for Princeton to be a down.

"It was actually a good thing that we finished with them. After the Yale game, we could easily have been let down and not ready to play. But as soon as Coach said, 'Penn,' we were ready to go. Of course, we expected they would feel the same way, especially after we found out how they had lost to Harvard."

The other two games would decide the top of the league.

Dartmouth had put together a remarkable season. When Teevens died in September shortly after a season-opening loss at New Hampshire, there was plenty of reason to believe it was going to be a long fall in Hanover.

"We weren't going to let that happen," running back Q Jones said. "We owed it to Coach T and ourselves to not let that happen. We had to keep going forward. We never felt sorry for ourselves. We had a lot of meetings before Josh [Balara] died and before Coach T's accident to talk about what had to be different in 2023 from 2022. We all thought that, as long as we focused on that and not on the tragedies, we'd be okay.

"We knew we had good players and we believed in the coaching staff. They deserve a lot of the credit for the way the season turned out."

After winning a very emotional home opener three days after Teevens died, the Big Green made the 360-mile trip from Hanover to Philadelphia and stunned Penn in overtime. Dartmouth had been picked sixth in the Ivy League in the preseason media poll, and there was plenty of talk about that in the locker room during halftime of the Penn game after the Big Green had taken a 20–10 lead.

"They picked us sixth, f— sixth," was the oft-repeated phrase while McCorkle was walking up and down amid the players while they relaxed.

"That was the game that told us we had a chance to do something special," McCorkle said. "Penn was good, we were on the road, and we had a lead and they came back. Then we won it in overtime."

The real turning point for Dartmouth—as for Princeton—had come in the Friday night game the first weekend in November when Owen Zalc kicked the game-winning field goal with 1:29 left to decide the game.

It wasn't a frigid night for Hanover in November—just a cold one—and with the game on over-the-air television (as opposed to streaming only), a tiny crowd of 2,526 showed up. Under the shadowy Memorial Field lights, the two teams staged a classic that many thousands would undoubtedly claim to have seen.

Both teams were 3–2 in the Ivy League walking off the field that night with two games left to play. The difference came the following week when Dartmouth, carrying all sorts of momentum, beat a fading Cornell team, 30–14, while Princeton lost to Yale.

That set up the final week. Harvard had clinched at least a tie for the title with its dramatic triple-overtime win over Penn. But if Yale were to beat Harvard and Dartmouth went to Brown and won, all three teams would finish 5–2.

"In the Ivy League, there are no tiebreakers," McCorkle said. "No one is going to postseason, so you don't have to declare one team the champion. You can have two champions or three. I don't think anyone complains."

Robin Harris, whose title is technically executive director but who is, in fact, the league's commissioner, agrees.

"If there's no reason to break a tie, why break it?" she said. "Let the players enjoy what they've accomplished by finishing first—or tied for first."

The Ivy League's first official season had been in 1956. In sixty-six seasons since then, there had been a tie for first place on twenty-four occasions—three of them involving three teams.

"Of course you want to win the title outright," Tim Murphy said. "But if you tie for the title, it's still sweet; it still gives the players the chance to celebrate a championship."

Only Murphy and Harvard had a chance win the title outright; Yale could share the title with a win over Harvard and Dartmouth needed a win at Brown and a Yale victory to make it a three-way tie. Yale had been picked first in the preseason poll and Harvard had been picked fourth. Dartmouth, as the players reminded each other frequently, had been picked sixth.

Yale and Harvard finishing at or near the top of the league was dog-bites-man stuff. Even though Dartmouth had won or shared more league championships than anyone (twenty), with Yale, Harvard, and Penn next at seventeen, Dartmouth had finished 3–7 in 2022 *before* the tragedies of 2023 had unfolded. That's why the Big Green had been picked sixth—ahead of only Columbia and Brown—and why their presence at the top of the league going into the last week was such a surprise.

"We definitely had our ups and downs all season," quarterback Nick Howard said. "But I don't think we ever got down on ourselves. It also helped when we found out that Coach McCorkle and the staff were going to be back. That was on our minds a lot until they made the decision that they were going to stay. We were all comfortable with that and we *knew* that was what Coach T would have wanted. It was what we all wanted. Once that happened, it was easier for us to just concentrate on football."

There was tangible evidence that Howard knew what he was talking about. On October 14, Dartmouth lost to Colgate in overtime to drop to 2–3 for the season.

Five days later, athletic director Mike Harrity announced that the "interim" tag was being removed from McCorkle's title. That meant the invisible interim title that was on the entire coaching staff was also removed.

David Shula had been a head coach in the NFL in the 1990s. He probably summed up the feelings of the staff best. He had left football for twenty-two years after leaving the Bengals but had been lured back into coaching by Teevens in 2018 when he convinced him to come back and coach his alma mater's wide receivers.

"We have an experienced staff here," he said. "I think most, if not all of us, could find jobs pretty easily if we had to. But none of us want to go any place else. We love it here. This is a unique place. That's why we have so much experience as a staff—no one looks to leave once they've been here. Knowing that Sammy's going to be the coach is a relief for all of us."

Somehow ending up sharing the title would be a major bonus for everyone. It was a long way from the tragedy of the spring and fall.

It was also a long way from sixth place.

## Chapter Twelve

AND THEN, THERE WAS THE GAME.

There are others that try to claim to be The Game in college football, but Yale-Harvard is *the* The Game.

Fans of Michigan and Ohio State will claim that their game is *the* game, but it wasn't played until 1897—twenty-two years after the first Yale-Harvard game. It has been played 119 times—twenty times fewer than Yale-Harvard. There's also The Big Game, contested between Stanford and Cal-Berkeley. That rivalry began five years prior to Ohio State-Michigan and has been played 126 times, including the famous "the band is on the field" game in 1983 that Cal won with five laterals on the final play of what was John Elway's last college game at Stanford.

Yale-Harvard is *not* the oldest rivalry in college football or the most frequently played. The oldest rivalry is Yale-Princeton, which began in 1873 and has been played 145 times. Lehigh-Lafayette has been played 159 times. Even though "The Rivalry," as it is called, wasn't played until 1884, the two schools met twice a year—and once *three* times in a season—until 1901.

The Game was actually called off in 1895 and 1896 after the 1894 game—a 12–4 Yale victory—became so violent that numerous players were hospitalized and fighting broke out in the streets of Springfield, Massachusetts, where the game was played.

In 1905, The Game and others had become so violent that President Theodore Roosevelt called for a White House meeting to discuss standardizing rules to make the sport less violent. Roosevelt, a Harvard graduate, loved football but was afraid the game might be banned if it remained as violent as it had become.

What probably saved football was the legalization of the forward pass in the early 1900s. It was John Heisman who pushed for the pass being legalized, pointing out that pass plays would open up the field and make the game less rugby-like and, thus, less violent. Heisman had played football for both Brown and Penn.

Harvard Stadium was built in the late 1800s and first hosted the Harvard-Yale game in 1903—won by Yale, 16–0. The Yale Bowl didn't open until 1914. It was truly a "bowl" with fans entering at the top of the bleachers and walking down to their seats since the stadium had literally been dug from beneath street level.

Many stadiums built in the next few years took the same approach, which is one reason why early postseason games were called "bowl games," starting most notably with the Rose Bowl.

When Harvard and Yale met in the Yale Bowl for the first time, two ex-presidents—Roosevelt and Yale graduate William Howard Taft—were in the building. Harvard won 36–0.

If there was one thing that Tim Murphy was most proud of among his accomplishments at Harvard, it was his 20–9 record against Yale. Between 2007 and 2015, Harvard won nine straight games, the longest streak for either school in the series.

But things began to change, albeit slowly, after Tony Reno arrived at Yale following the 2011 season. Reno was working for Murphy when the chance to take over Yale's program popped up. Reno had worked for seven seasons at Yale under Coach Jack Siedlecki, who had gone 70–49 in twelve seasons after replacing the legendary Carmen Cozza, who had coached at Yale for thirty-one seasons.

Yale won the Ivy League title in 2006 and went 9–1 in 2007, but when the record dropped to 6–4 in 2008, many alumni were upset. Feeling the pressure, Siedlecki announced he was "retiring" at the age of fifty-seven. He was replaced by Tom Williams, a Stanford graduate with an impressive résumé, including being a candidate for a Rhodes Scholarship.

Williams was only the second Black head coach for an Ivy League football team (following Norries Wilson, who had coached Columbia for five seasons beginning in 2005).

Williams brought in a new coaching staff, leaving Reno without a job. He contacted Murphy to see if he had an opening—and he did. Three years later, Williams's stint at Yale ended suddenly. In doing a story in 2011 on Yale quarterback Patrick Witt, who had been selected as a Rhodes Scholarship finalist, the *New York Times* discovered that Williams had not been a Rhodes candidate and that his claim that he had been on the San Francisco 49ers practice squad was also untrue.

Williams's attempts to explain the deceptions were quite weak: he claimed that two Stanford professors had *recommended* that he apply for a Rhodes but he never got around to doing it. He also said he'd gone to a three-day tryout camp with the 49ers but never signed a contract.

Witt ended up having to choose between playing The Game in 2011 or going to his Rhodes interview since both were on the same day. He chose to play and Harvard won, 45–7, wrapping up an undefeated season. Yale finished 5–5 and six weeks later, Williams resigned, ending up six weeks after that as an assistant coach for the University of Texas at El Paso.

Reno had been successful as an assistant coach at both Yale and Harvard and was still only thirty-seven years old. He was interested in the vacant head coaching job at Yale; ultimately, Yale decided his background coaching and recruiting Ivy League players made him the ideal person for the job.

After suffering through a 2–8 season in 2012, Reno's second team went 5–5, and his third team was 8–2. In 2016, Yale ended Harvard's nine-game winning streak in The Game. A year later, the Bulldogs went 9–1 and won the league title for the first time since 2006. It then tied for the title with Dartmouth in 2019 and won outright in 2022, thanks to a win over then-undefeated Princeton and a victory in The Game, played at Harvard.

Having coached at both schools, Reno was extremely conscious of the importance of The Game, regardless of either team's record. When he had first arrived at Yale, Reno insisted that Harvard be referred to as "The Team from the North," a steal from Ohio State, which always referred to Michigan that way. There was no reference to Harvard on the schedules that hung from the walls in the Yale football offices—only, "The Team from the North."

"I wanted to make it clear that Harvard was not *the* team in The Game," Reno said with a grin. "I thought that was one small way to do it."

Of course the other way to do it was to actually win The Game. Starting in 2016, Yale began to do that, winning four of the next six games, including a remarkable 50–43 overtime win in 2019. The Bulldogs scored two touchdowns in the final eighty-eight seconds to tie the game at 36–36, then won the game in the second overtime when they scored and stopped Harvard on fourth down. Many Yalies declared that the comeback—which allowed Yale to tie Dartmouth for the league title—was the equal of Harvard's 29–29 "victory" in 1968.

That game ended in the dark, leading to Yale putting in permanent lights—thirteen years after Harvard had put lights into Harvard Stadium.

The only thing the 2019 game lacked was a brilliant student newspaper headline.

Yale had won The Game at Harvard in 2022 to clinch the league title.

"Standing on their field waiting to hear the final score of Princeton-Penn was one of the most thrilling experiences of my life," said Yale captain Wande Owens. "We were celebrating because we'd won at Harvard and because we knew that—at worst—we would tie for the title. When we heard that Penn had won, it just topped off the day and the whole season. It's a great memory we'll always have."

Harvard was hoping to do to Yale what Yale had done to it when the teams met in the Yale Bowl on the afternoon of November 18, 2023.

It was the proverbial perfect afternoon for a football game. The day had started off rainy but had cleared off in time for the noon kickoff. There were still some clouds in the sky, but the temperature was a balmy—for November in Connecticut—fifty degrees.

The Yale Bowl once seated seventy thousand, but the capacity had been reduced to a little over sixty thousand during a 2006 renovation. Ivy League games average about ten thousand fans per week during the rest of the season, but Yale-Harvard is usually a sellout or close to it, regardless of where it is played.

Harvard Stadium once seated as many as fifty-seven thousand fans, but renovations took the official capacity down to twenty-five thousand—although the official attendance for the 2022 game is listed as 30,006.

The stadium didn't appear to be close to sold out when the game began. There were patches of empty seats on the Yale side and large swaths with no fans on the Harvard side. The reason was Yale's computer ticketing system had suffered major glitches, causing long lines of fans (with tickets) trying to get into the stadium. It wasn't until midway in the second quarter that the 51,121 who would just about fill the stadium were able to get to their seats.

Harvard-Yale is unique in many ways, not the least of which is the toss of the coin. It may be the only college football game in which each team sends out only one captain. Just about every team in college football has multiple captains. The tradition at Harvard and Yale is to elect one captain at the team's award banquets that take place right after the season ends.

Harvard's captain was defensive end Nate Leskovec, an intense Ohioan who had been overwhelmingly elected by his teammates on both sides of the ball. Although Leskovec was quiet by nature, he was the kind of leader everyone on the team looked up to and respected both on and off the field.

"I know it's tradition and I understand it," Leskovec said. "But I think it's tough for one guy to worry about his own play, the play of both units, and the mentality of the entire team. It's an unbelievable honor and I don't see it changing. I was lucky because unofficially [offensive tackle] Jake Rizy was my co-captain. He's a natural leader."

Yale captain Wande Owens was more outgoing, easygoing off the field, competitive as hell on the field. When his teammates made their traditional "Bulldog Walk" from the locker room to the pre-game prep room inside the stadium, Owens stood outside the door and hugged everyone as they walked into the room.

Like Harvard Stadium, the Yale Bowl had no actual locker rooms. New locker rooms were being built during the 2023 season, which meant that Yale's players and coaches dressed and prepared in trailers that were outside the gates to the stadium. The new locker rooms would be inside the stadium gates, closer to the team's prep room, but still about a 200-yard walk away.

The visiting prep room was directly across the field from the Yale prep room and was also in a trailer—much like the visiting locker room at Harvard. The biggest issue for both teams: finding enough time and space for everyone to get a bathroom break at halftime.

Needless to say, this was not an issue when Ohio State played their own "Team from the North."

While Harvard's fans were trying to get to their seats, their players were struggling to get their feet under them on the field.

After forcing Yale to punt to start the game, the Crimson moved to the Yale 45 with a first down. But the Yale defense stopped quarterback Jaden Craig on a fourth-and-three at the 38 and the Bulldogs took over on the 37. From there they slowly marched to the Harvard 15, picking up four consecutive third downs and using sixteen plays to move 48 yards. When the Harvard defense got a stop, Jack Bosman kicked a 33-yard-field goal to give Yale a 3–0 lead with less than a minute to go in the first quarter.

Harvard followed the field goal with a disastrous series. On third-and-nine, Craig was sacked by Ezekiel Larry for a 16-yard loss that pushed the ball back to the 16. Then Sebastien Tasko got off an uncharacteristically poor punt, the ball going out of bounds on the Harvard 41.

Yale couldn't move the ball from there, but Bosman punted the ball to the 14 and Harvard started at the 15 after a 1-yard return. Harvard picked up one first down, but then Larry *again* sacked Craig for a 10-yard loss back to the 19. This time, Tasko's punt was blocked by Wyatt Raymond and recovered at the 7 by Zion Dayne.

From there, Yale needed just three plays to get into the end zone. On third down from the 5, quarterback Nolan Grooms stepped up in the pocket and found Ryan Lindley over the middle for the touchdown.

It was 10–0 Yale with 9:12 left until halftime. The Yale side of the field was buoyant. Even with most fans finally in their seats, the Harvard side was almost silent.

The Harvard sideline was calm. Tim Murphy's teams rarely panicked, even in the biggest game of any year. On the defensive bench, Leskovec, in a very calm voice, said to his teammates, "We're fine guys. There's a lot of football left. No need to panic."

They didn't, although it took a while and some heroic work by the defense to get the Crimson going.

Craig was intercepted, but the defense held. Then Tasko had another punt blocked—but the defense sacked Grooms twice, moving the ball back from the 7 yard line to the 29. On the second sack, Grooms fumbled, and linebacker Matt Hudson recovered at Harvard's 41. In all, the Crimson defense had pushed the ball 34 yards away from the goal line in the wake of the Craig interception.

From there, the Crimson offense finally got going. Three big plays got Harvard on the scoreboard. First, running back Shane McLaughlin shook loose for 15 yards, the first big running play of the game for the Crimson. Then Craig, who had taken a beating throughout the half, found Kaedyn Odermann open deep over the middle at the Yale 9. Finally, with 1:08 left on the clock, Craig hit Tyler Neville over the middle for a touchdown that closed the gap to 10–6.

Cali Canaval's extra point was blocked—the Harvard special teams were having a rough half—and the score remained 10–6. Still, there was a clear momentum switch with Harvard finally being on the board.

Yale had one last brief possession, but it ended when—appropriately enough—Leskovec sacked Grooms to end the half. It was Harvard's fourth sack of the half, a major reason that they were only down four points, even though Yale had blocked two punts, gotten an interception, and dominated most of the first thirty minutes.

Thirty minutes to go. Thirty minutes left in The Game. Thirty minutes left in the season. Thirty minutes left to decide whether a championship would be outright or shared.

And, in the case of many of the seniors, thirty minutes left to play football.

That was the basic message from both coaches to their players during the halftime break.

Thirty minutes.

Among the 262 Division I college football teams—134 FBS and 128 FCS—only the eight Ivy League teams begin the season knowing it will end exactly ten weeks later. FBS teams play a twelve-game regular season and eighty-two of them play in a postseason game. With conference championship victories and two games each in the College Football Playoff, both Michigan and Washington played fifteen games in 2023–2024. In the FCS, the regular season is eleven games long, and twenty-four teams play at least one game in the postseason tournament. The two tournament finalists play four extra games, occasionally five.

Not the Ivy League. "It's a sprint and a marathon at the same time," Harvard's All-Ivy offensive tackle Jake Rizy said. "On the one hand, you feel like the Yale game comes about five minutes after you open the season. It just whizzes past you. On the other hand, there are no bye weeks, no chance to catch your breath once you get started. It's exhausting. By the end of the season, every team has guys playing who are hurt one way or another."

The Ivy League season lasts exactly sixty-three days from the first Saturday until the last. Most FBS schools, who have eighty-five scholarships each, have seasons that last at least thirteen weeks—or ninety-one days. In 2023 Navy's season lasted fifteen weeks—105 days—from start to finish. None of those numbers include postseason.

One of the reasons Columbia's Al Bagnoli decide to retire before the 2023 season began was the grind of the Ivy League season.

"Basically you work every day for fifteen straight weeks beginning with preseason," Bagnoli said. "After my heart procedure [in March], I just didn't feel I had the energy at seventy to do it again. I'd done it for thirty straight years. I decided to not put myself through that again."

Harvard's Tim Murphy knew all about health issues. Early in 2014, while watching television at home with his wife, Martha, he had a heart attack. Fortunately, Murphy recognized the symptoms and got right to a hospital. He missed none of spring practice—which is why his visit to Buddy Teevens in September had been his first missed practice in forty-five years—and Harvard had gone 10–0 that season and 9–1 in 2015.

Murphy had been fifty-eight when he had his heart attack—twelve years younger than Bagnoli. That certainly made a difference.

Once he recovered, Murphy became a physical fitness fanatic. He was up at five thirty every morning, rode his bicycle to his office, went for a swim, and then rode his bike every day at lunch time. He was fit, trim, and still full of energy.

But there was no doubt that Teevens's death affected him emotionally. The plan to retire together was now gone, and Murphy had become more of a loner than in the past. His pregame routine was to shake hands and say hello to the opposing coach and the officials and then to walk around the field by himself. He was polite to anyone he encountered, but it was clear he preferred to be alone with his thoughts in the hour before the game.

Reno, who had once coached under Murphy, was much the same. Always friendly and polite, it was clear his mind was on the game long before kickoff.

Now the two men and their teams had thirty minutes left to play to try to make all the work pay off before another long offseason began.

Yale struck first midway through the third quarter, driving 47 yards in nine plays, Nathan Denney scoring from 4 yards out after Grooms had found Ryan Lindley for 17 yards on a third-and-seven to set up the score.

Just when it looked as if Yale had control of the game with a 17–6 lead, Harvard's offense finally showed up. After the Crimson had struggled for almost three quarters to move the ball at all, it suddenly exploded. Taking over at its own 42, it went 58 yards in five plays. Shane McLaughlin opened the drive with a 20-yard run, Harvard's longest of the day. Then, Craig found Cooper Barkate across the middle for 28 yards to the Yale 10. The Harvard bench was suddenly alive.

Three plays later, on the first play of the fourth quarter, Craig outran the Yale defense from the 7 to the corner of the end zone and it was 17–12. Trying to make up for the first-half missed extra point, the Crimson went for two and failed. It remained 17–12 with almost the entire fourth quarter still to play.

Joshua Pitsenberger, who would finish with 99 rushing yards, picked up 10 yards for a quick first down for Yale, but then the Harvard defense forced a punt and the Crimson began on their own 42 yard line *again*.

This time, Craig found Barkate—who would finish with four catches for 60 yards—to open the drive, with a 30-yard strike that moved the ball to the Yale 28. Four plays and one penalty later, Craig found Ledger Hatch from 7 yards out and, suddenly, shockingly, Harvard had the lead, 18–17—even after another missed two-point conversion.

Now it was Yale's turn to find its offense. The key play was a 31-yard completion to Mason Tipton that put the ball on the Harvard 40. Grooms then ran three straight times for 23 yards to the Harvard 17. But on second-and-seven, Harvard came with a blitz and, struggling to find space or a receiver, Grooms forced a pass that was intercepted by Damien Henderson at the Harvard 7.

There was 7:42 on the clock and control of the game had clearly swung to Harvard. On first down, McLaughlin picked up 2 yards.

Then came the key play of a game filled with key plays.

Craig scrambled away from what looked like a certain sack and picked up 6 yards, setting up what would have been a third-and-short. But as Craig was being dragged down by a host of tacklers,

Joseph Vaughn reached in and slapped the ball loose. In a wild scramble, Osize Daniyan, a freshman defensive back from Mount Juliet, Tennessee, ended up on top of it at the Harvard 14.

Now, Yale had about as short a field as you could possibly ask for and the Bulldogs quickly took advantage as the already-winded Harvard defense came back on the field almost before anybody had a chance to sit down after celebrating Henderson's interception.

The Crimson tried, hoping to hold Yale to a field goal. But after two Pitsenberger runs picked up only 2 yards, Grooms found David Pantelis on a swing pass to the right, and Pantelis dove into the end zone for the touchdown.

Hoping to stretch the lead to seven, Yale went for two, but the defense kept Pitsenberger from reaching the end zone and the score was 23–18 with 5:47 still left to play.

Time was now a factor. Harvard started at the 25 after a touchback on the kickoff, and Craig quickly hit Barkate yet again, this time for 17 yards to that familiar spot, the Harvard 42.

Craig came right back and completed a short pass on the right side to Tim Dowd, who dodged several tacklers and wasn't brought down until he reached the Yale 14. At the very least, Harvard was in field goal range with lots of time on the clock.

But a touchdown was needed to take the lead back. This time it was the Yale defense that stiffened with the ball near the goal line. After Craig completed a pass to Barkate to move the ball to the 6, setting up third-and-two, he twice threw incomplete to Barkate. On the fourth-down pass, Craig had to run right to escape Abu Kamara and threw the ball beyond Barkate's reach.

Yale took over with 3:36 left needing two first downs to put the game away.

It got one. Pitsenberger picked up 13 yards on first down, moving the ball to the 19. But the next three plays netted one yard and Yale had to punt again.

A short punt to the Yale 45 gave Harvard the ball one last time with 1:47 on the clock and one time-out left.

Three short passes later, the Crimson had a first down at the 29. But Yale came with a blitz and sacked Craig for an 11-yard loss, moving the ball back to the 40 with 1:17 left.

Harvard took its last time-out to try to deal with second-and-twenty-one. Two more short passes—one incomplete and one good for 7 yards—left Harvard facing fourth-and-fourteen from the 33. This time, Yale called time-out—with forty-six seconds left—to be sure everyone on defense knew what they were doing.

"They didn't have to score," Wande Owens said. "But a first down inbounds meant they'd probably have time for one more play since they were out of time-outs. We wanted to keep guys in front of us."

They almost didn't. Craig had some time, but as the rush closed in, he stepped up and threw deep in the left corner to Barkate, who appeared to have a step on Sean Guyton. But, throwing on the run after stepping up in the pocket and trying to be sure he would get the ball over Guyton's hands, Craig put a little too much on the pass. It flew about six inches over Barkate's outstretched hands.

"He was open," Murphy said later. "It was there. Jaden just put a little too much on the ball. If he'd had an extra second, I think he'd have gotten the ball there. But he didn't. He showed a lot of poise on the play to get the pass off and in the direction of the right guy. He needed to make a perfect play. He just didn't quite make it."

One kneel down from Grooms later, the clock finally hit zero and The Game was over. Final score: Yale 23, Harvard 18.

The emotions spilled over quickly. The players and coaches exchanged hugs and handshakes. A faux championship trophy was brought out so the Yale players could enjoy tying for the title.

In Providence, 192 miles away, Dartmouth and Brown had finished their game eleven minutes earlier than Harvard and Yale. The Dartmouth players stayed on the field to celebrate the win and to wait to hear a final score from New Haven.

"I thought about telling everyone to go into the locker room while we waited," Coach Sammy McCorkle said later. "But then I said, 'Heck with it,' let's just stay out here and enjoy what we've done, regardless of the outcome at Yale. It was a nice day so there was no need to get inside. I didn't look at my phone because I was too nervous. But then I heard a bunch of shouting and I realized we'd done it."

Yale's victory meant that there was a three-way tie at the top of the league—Harvard, Yale, and Dartmouth, all at 5–2. Harvard had finished 8–2 overall, Yale 7–3, and Dartmouth 6–4. But the overall record didn't matter; the 5–2 mattered.

Another faux trophy was brought on to the field at Brown, and McCorkle led the informal victory parade, trophy held high in the air.

"What an amazing story," Cornell's Dave Archer said later. "He went from coach *for* a year to coach *of* the year. I couldn't be happier for him and for his team, especially after all they went through."

Archer and Mark Fabish had both coached their last games that day. Each was disappointed, though in different ways. Fabish honestly believed he deserved more time, especially given the circumstances in which he'd gotten the job—six weeks before the start of the season.

Archer had been given ten years at Cornell, arguably the toughest school for a coach to win at in the Ivy League. Al Bagnoli had engineered a remarkable turnaround at Columbia but would be the first to say that budget and facilities improvements had helped him immensely. Archer got no such concessions but understood that ten years was a lot of time.

"We were 5–5 a year ago and that was an improvement," he said. "But I knew coming into the season it was up or out. We were 3–7 and that meant out. I've devoted most of my adult life to Cornell football, so it hurts. But I'm not going to leave pointing the finger at anyone. Even if I did, it wouldn't change anything."

Archer and Fabish weren't the only coaches who would be leaving. The difference was that Tim Murphy was going to leave voluntarily after thirty-one years at Harvard.

Even though Murphy insisted he hadn't made a final decision after The Game was over, there were all sorts of clues, especially if you'd watched him struggle emotionally through the season after Teevens's death.

Murphy was never one to get overly emotional in the locker room whether in victory or defeat—other than his joy when he got to do the Murphy Leap.

He was brief when he spoke to his players after the Yale loss but clearly emotional.

"The only thing I ever ask from one of my teams is 100 percent effort every day," he said. "You guys have given me that and more. Losing today is sad, but we're still Ivy League champions and let's enjoy that because you earned it."

He then worked his way around the room hugging people, telling them he loved them and thanking them. There was much hugging in the room and plenty of tears—not so much for the loss as for the ending.

"Four years of football seem to pass in a heartbeat," said Leskovec, who was one of the last players to leave the room. I know that's the way most guys feel. But when it's actually over, it hits you pretty hard."

"In a very real way, you don't want to leave that room," Logan Bednar said. "Because when you do, it hits you that it's over—football is over. After you've played most of your life, that's something that hits you very hard."

"If you don't get emotional about it, something is wrong," Jake Rizy said. "I knew I was going to play football again, but not for Harvard. It was going to feel different."

Murphy, who had been coaching for forty-five years, understood those feelings. And he felt a lot of those same emotions as he stood by the door and hugged one player after another (often for a second time) as they left.

"The last play was *so* close," he said. "Cooper had the step, Jaden saw him, but he didn't have quite the time he needed to make an accurate throw." His eyes were still misty. "So close."

There were similar emotions in the Yale locker room, especially for the seniors—but the joy of achieving what had seemed virtually impossible six weeks into the season made for a much happier atmosphere.

Most players and coaches stayed on the field once the Harvard players left for the thirty minutes designated for fans to come onto the field and join in the postgame party. Gradually, they worked their way to the ramp and the steps leading to the postgame meeting room. Cigars were handed out and, by the time Reno got to the locker room, the air was filled with cigar smoke.

One of the many traditions of Yale-Harvard is that there is no trophy—just the game ball. Reno walked in and presented it to

Owens—the captain. Then he told his players how proud he was and what it meant to beat The Team from the North, regardless of the standings. Tying for the league title by winning was an added bonus.

When they finally trickled out, most still puffing on their cigars, the sun was slowly starting to set. There would be plenty of parties and celebrations that night before all Ivy League players would start to head home for Thanksgiving. Just about the only good thing about the Ivy League school presidents' silly rule banning the football champion from playing in postseason was that the players all got to be home for Thanksgiving.

Even so, the Yale players no doubt felt a pang of jealousy watching their basketball team win the league's championship tournament in March and then stun fourth-seeded Auburn in the first round of the NCAA Tournament. That's exactly the kind of glory the football players felt capable of achieving but were denied the chance to prove.

"I've coached in the league for twenty years," Reno said. "I think the best team we've had in those years was Princeton in 2018. If they'd had the chance to play postseason, I honestly think they were good enough to win the whole thing. Not a game or two, the whole thing."

Princeton's Bob Surace doesn't disagree. "We were very good," he said. "Would we have won the whole thing? Who knows?" He smiled. "But it would have been nice to take a crack at it."

# Chapter Thirteen

AND SO, AS THE FIFTY-ONE-THOUSAND-PLUS fans fought their way out of the Yale Bowl parking lots, the sun set on another Ivy League season.

Harvard, Yale, and Dartmouth became the fourth tri-champions in league history. Their 5–2 records marked only the fourth time in sixty-seven seasons that every team in the league had lost at least two conference games.

Tim Murphy took some solace in the fact that Harvard was the only one of the champions without a nonleague loss. Harvard also had the most impressive nonleague win: its victory over then-fourth ranked (in the FCS poll) Holy Cross in early October.

Princeton, after its devastating overtime loss to Yale, won at Penn in the teams' finale to finish fourth at 4–3. The Quakers finished 3–4, tied with Brown for fifth. Cornell, which had started conference play at 2–0, finished 2–5, and Columbia finally won a game in the final weekend of the season when it went to Cornell and won, 29–14, to finish 1–6.

The biggest surprise, of course, was Dartmouth, picked sixth—as the players liked to point out—in the preseason. With all due respect to Harvard and Yale, the Big Green had to be the story of the year for reasons both tragic and remarkable.

Coming off a 3–7 season (2–5 in league play) and reversing that mark to tie for first, was a story by itself. But doing it after a player—Josh Balara—had died of cancer and the school's longtime head coach, Buddy Teevens, had died after being hit by a truck while riding his bicycle was beyond sad, heartwarming, and stunning.

Throw in the fact that no one knew until mid-October who would ultimately replace Teevens—Sammy McCorkle—and Dartmouth's season becomes something straight out of a Disney movie.

"What those players and coaches did was something they should all be proud of for the rest of their lives," Harvard coach Tim Murphy said. "You can't possibly give them all enough credit for what they accomplished in the midst of two major tragedies."

McCorkle didn't move into Teevens's office until the season was over, feeling like it still belonged to his old boss, even after athletic director Mike Harrity removed the interim tag from his title. Only when the season was over and some renovation work had been done did he move in. "Still feels a little strange," he said in December. "It will be hard to not think of this as Coach T's office."

While McCorkle and his team were creating their Disney movie, Cornell and Columbia were looking for new coaches as soon as the season ended. Both moved quickly. Columbia hired Jon Poppe, who had familiarity with elite academic schools having played at Williams as a defensive back and having coached at Harvard (twice) and at Columbia, including being part of Al Bagnoli's 8–2 staff in 2017.

Poppe turned thirty-nine shortly after being hired. He had left Harvard to become the head coach at Division 3 Union in 2023 and had gone 10–2, reaching the second round of the D-3 tournament.

"This is a very comfortable move for me," Poppe said. "I know people at Columbia, I know my way around the city, I know the kind of kids we need to recruit to have success here.

"There's certainly talent here. They were very close in a lot of games last season. We have to figure out how to turn those results around."

Cornell stayed inside the Ivy League, hiring Penn offensive coordinator Dan Swanstrom. Like Poppe, Swanstrom was young—forty-one—but Cornell was not his first head coaching job. In fact, Cornell was a return home for Swanstrom since he had been the head coach at Ithaca University for five years and had gone 32–11. He had come to Ithaca from Penn and then returned to Penn as the offensive coordinator in 2022.

Swanstrom had been a star quarterback at Division 3 Rhodes College in Tennessee and had coached high school ball for one year in Texas before coaching at the college level. His quarterback at Stratford High School was Andrew Luck—yes, *that* Andrew Luck.

Swanstrom loved Penn, loved Philadelphia, and loved working for Ray Priore for a second time.

"This is like a dream job for me," he said during the 2023 season. "I love the kids I coach, I love the guy I work for, and I love the school. I couldn't be happier with what I do than I am right now."

But the chance to be the head coach at an Ivy League school in a place he was familiar with proved irresistible to Swanstrom. A lot of coaches would no doubt shy away from Cornell, which last had a winning season in 2005. There was no doubt how hard Dave Archer had worked during his ten years as coach, or about his love for Cornell, but his record had been 29–71.

Swanstrom will need help with facilities and in fundraising if he is going to turn Cornell around, but, like Poppe, he goes into his new job with both enthusiasm and hope. In Swanstrom's case, he would seem to be an ideal coach for Jameson Wang, whose potential as he enters his senior season still feels as if it hasn't yet been tapped entirely.

What was more surprising than the coaching turnover was the coaching stability in the league prior to 2023. At the end of the 2022 season, Brown's James Perry had the least experience on the job—four years, including only three playing seasons because of the COVID wipeout of 2020. Tim Murphy had been at Harvard for thirty years; Buddy Teevens had been back at Dartmouth for seventeen years; Princeton's Bob Surace had been on the job for thirteen years; Yale's Tony Reno had finished his eleventh year at Yale; Dave Archer had been at Cornell for nine years; Penn's Ray Priore had been in charge for eight years; and Al Bagnoli had been at Columbia for eight years—after twenty-three seasons at Penn.

Four of the eight coaches—Perry, Teevens, Surace, and Archer—were coaching at the school where they had played. A year later, only Perry and Surace remained.

In all, three of the coaches who had finished 2022 were gone: Teevens due to tragedy, Bagnoli due to health issues, and Archer due to lack of wins.

And there was still one more change—the most significant one—to come.

As was tradition, both Harvard and Yale had their team banquets right after the season had ended—Yale on campus in its tennis center; Harvard in downtown Boston at The Harvard Club. Yale's banquet was on Sunday; Harvard's on Monday. It was also tradition to announce the following season's team captains at those banquets as voted by the players, meaning there wasn't much time to collect and count the votes.

Yale elected linebacker Dean Shaffer, who had come a long way since his senior season at East Smithtown (Long Island) High School when he had only been able to play in one game because of injuries.

Harvard elected a player from the offensive side of the ball for the first time since 2007, when the players elected All-Ivy running back Shane McLaughlin.

Tim Murphy had thought of retirement more in the abstract prior to 2023 than thinking about an exact date when he might walk away. He was in the enviable position of knowing the decision would be his whenever the time came.

His record at Harvard, going into the 2023 season—192–87, including nine Ivy League titles—spoke for itself. He wasn't just Harvard's winningest coach, he was the Ivy League's winningest coach. That and the fact that he was so respected in football circles made him the FCS's answer to Alabama's Nick Saban.

Saban retired at the age of seventy-two at the end of the 2023 season in the wake of a semifinal playoff loss (in overtime) to eventual national champion Michigan. Saban had an overall record of 292–71–1. As far as people in Alabama were concerned, Saban could have coached until he was one hundred if he had chosen to do so.

Murphy's status at Harvard was the same as Saban's at Alabama. He won a lot of games, and he did it with good kids who were good students—almost all Harvard football players, stars and nonstars, graduated.

That was true, of course, across the entire league. "Even if you *knew* you were going to play ten years in the NFL, you'd be wasting an opportunity to get an Ivy League degree if you didn't focus on the academics," Princeton's Jalen Travis said. "You have to understand that you have two full-time jobs: football and academics. It's not easy to get everything done that you need to get done, but you know in the end if you do what you need to do, it'll be worth it. The football is short term; the academics are long term."

Murphy had turned sixty-seven on October 9—eight days after Teevens would have turned sixty-seven and twenty days after his death—and had retirement on his mind throughout the season. "I'm not going to be coaching when I'm seventy," he said one fall morning. "But that doesn't mean I don't have a couple more years left in me. I honestly don't know what I'm going to do at this point."

The fact that the team had such a good season made the idea of walking away a little easier to deal with. Prior to the Christmas holidays, he still wasn't sure. Finally, he sat down with his number-one adviser—his wife, Martha—to talk the whole thing through.

"There were a lot of numbers that seemed to fall into place for me to retire," he said later. "I'd won my two hundredth game at Harvard when we beat Penn and clinched my tenth Ivy League title when we did that. We did it in the 150th year of Harvard football. I'd coached at Harvard for thirty years. It felt like serendipity—just a lot of zeros there to talk about.

"And then there was Buddy. We had talked for as long as I can remember about the fact that when it was time, we'd go out together. I think the first time we actually discussed it was when I was at Maine in the early nineties and he was at Stanford. I thought about that every day during the season. I thought about Buddy every day, I couldn't help it. I was in touch with Kirsten almost every day.

"I didn't want to just walk away right after the Yale game. That was the wrong time to make a decision like that. We were inches away from winning that game, but we didn't win it. Still, we did win a championship and we did have the best record in the league.

"We came into the season with a chip on our shoulder. We weren't used to finishing fourth in the league (2022) or being picked fourth in the preseason. That certainly got our attention. The players are well aware of our history in football and they're proud of it. So am I."

Like most coaches, Murphy tended to focus on the losses more than the wins.

"I thought we could pass the ball against Princeton," he said. "We couldn't. Their defense did a great job, and it took us almost three quarters to get going. Yale was a great football game. We made some key mistakes and so did they. We just missed converting that last pass by inches."

Harvard decided to go outside of the staff in its coaching search and, less than four weeks after Murphy announced his retirement, the school hired a Princeton graduate, Andrew Aurich, who had been a Princeton assistant under Bob Surace, before spending three years at Rutgers. Not long after taking the job, Aurich announced that he was retaining most of Murphy's coaching staff—ten coaches in all.

That decision made players and ex-players happy. Even so, they had been surprised and disappointed when the new coach hadn't been someone on the staff. Most had assumed that whenever Murphy retired, his successor would be either defensive coordinator Scott Larkee—a 1999 graduate who had played for Murphy—or offensive coordinator Mickey Fein—also class of '99, but from Maine—who had been on the staff for eight years.

"I know I'm biased because I played on the defensive side of the ball, but I always thought Coach Larkee would be and should be the choice," Leskovec said. "He's a Harvard guy, he's a terrific coach, and it just made the most sense to me for him to follow Coach Murphy.

"This is nothing against Coach Aurich. Everything I've heard from guys since he took over has been positive. We had a group of former captains [the last four] who talked among ourselves about what we might do to see to it that Coach Larkee got the job. It didn't work out. I think it says something positive though that he kept so much of the staff around—including Coach Larkee."

The three new head coaches hired within the league after the 2023 season were all relatively young: Aurich was forty, Swanstrom was forty-one, and Poppe was thirty-nine. In what felt like a heartbeat, James Perry went from the league's least experienced coach to ranking fourth behind only Surace, Reno, and Priore. In 2024 there would be three coaches in their first season, one in his second season (McCorkle), Perry in his fifth season, and then came the three "old men."

"Bob Surace and I were walking into a coaches meeting in January," Reno said. "For years, we had been the kids in the room. Being around those guys with all that experience was a learning experience for us. Even though we were competing with them, they were our mentors in very real ways. That day, Bob and I looked at each other and said, 'Holy Cow, we're the old men now. How did that happen?'"

Reno and Surace both believe that Murphy and Bagnoli are locks to be in the College Football Hall of Fame and that Teevens also belongs there. Those three combined to win 652 games as college coaches—Bagnoli 269, Murphy 234, and Teevens, who had two stints at FBS schools, 151.

The biggest change in the league though is what many players are doing when their Ivy League playing careers are over. Because of the COVID year, all NCAA players were granted a fifth year of eligibility. Others, who have been injured, can also get a fifth year—and, in some cases, a sixth year—just not in the Ivy League. They can't use the fifth year as graduate students at the school where they played for four years because Ivy League rules prohibit graduate students, regardless of their academic status.

This has always been an Ivy League rule. You can compete in sports for a total of eight semesters. Being a *good* student, finishing your degree on time or sooner, is actually a disadvantage in terms of eligibility.

Some players who wanted to play during their fifth fall dropped out of school to maintain their status as undergraduates, so they could come back for an extra season of football. For some reason, the Ivy League has always frowned on players who have graduated but have eligibility left from playing another year. Why exactly the league wouldn't want players who have graduated pursuing a master's degree is difficult to understand.

"I think the way they look at it is, 'We gave you a golden ticket as an undergraduate, should we give you another golden ticket to go to grad school?'" Leskovec said. "I understand why they might feel that way."

And so, at the end of the 2023 season, the number of players who had finished their eligibility at an Ivy League school but still were eligible to play at an FBS school was more than it had ever been.

Joey Slackman, the league's defensive player of the year at Penn, was pursued by more than thirty schools. He ended up choosing to take his talents—as LeBron James might say—to Florida. Princeton's Ozzie Nicholas, who finished second to Slackman for the defensive award, chose Duke—knowing that a big-time transfer quarterback, Texas's Maalik Murphy, had committed to go there. Duke also signed Slackman's teammate Will Seiler.

Because Jalen Travis had missed half the season with his ankle injury, his draft status had become more questionable so he decided to be a grad transfer and chose Iowa State—which is in the Big 12 and would allow him to play a little more than two hundred miles from his home in Minneapolis.

Harvard's Tyler Neville chose Virginia among his many suitors. Jacob Rizy, the All-Ivy offensive tackle, went to Florida State; linebacker Matt Hudson, who was voted the team's MVP, chose Memphis. In all, seven Harvard players transferred in order to play an extra year.

Leskovec, who was one of three Harvard players granted a fifth year because of COVID—although he had to take a semester off in order to remain an undergraduate during the fall of 2023—knew the Yale game would be his last as a football player.

"I suppose I could have given playing in the NFL a shot, but I honestly don't think I was good enough," he said. "I was a good player, but I wasn't an NFL-caliber player. I played with NFL-caliber players and played against them too. I just didn't think I was at that level."

Leskovec was offered the chance to be part of the Ivy League all-star team that traveled to Japan after the season to play a team of Japanese all-stars. The game was the second "Dream Japan Bowl." The Ivy League had won the first game a year earlier but lost the second game in January of 2024.

Columbia's Al Bagnoli had coached the first team and brought along fifteen of his players. Brown's James Perry coached the second team and brought twelve Bears with him.

Leskovec turned down the chance to go to Japan.

"I knew it would be cool and the guys who went told me they had a great time," he said. "But I had decided I wanted my last game to be in a Harvard uniform. It just felt like the right thing to do. Of course I'd have preferred that we beat Yale, but I still walked away feeling I'd been blessed to go to Harvard and to play football for Harvard and get a degree from Harvard. I mean, I could not have been luckier."

He paused. "Of course, losing to Yale sucked."

Leskovec graduated in December with a degree in economics and was hired right away by a Boston firm called Summit Partners as a growth equity tech analyst. He had cut his long blond hair into a crewcut before the season began and kept it that way right through the Yale game.

"I wanted a kind of warrior look," he said, laughing. "I wanted to look tough when I played and when I went out for the toss of the coin. As soon as the season ended, I let my hair grow back. I'm still waiting [this was in late March] for someone to suggest I cut it. But I do look like myself again."

All the players who would be grad transfers would leave their Ivy League schools with degrees. Some, who had graduated in December, were on their new campuses for spring practice. Others, who would graduate in May or June, passed on spring practice to stick around to get their degree.

"It is different," Surace said. "When I played, you had four years, you graduated, and you moved on with your life. Now, so many kids have eligibility and they want to pursue playing football, it's different. A lot of them are playing their senior years hoping to set themselves up to move to the FBS level and perhaps from there to the NFL. And there's absolutely nothing wrong with that kind of thing."

Ozzie Nicholas was a perfect example of that. "The truth is, if I hadn't had two knee surgeries [both ACLs] in high school, I would have gone to an FBS school. I had plenty of interest until I got hurt. Being from the West Coast [San Diego], there were a lot of Pac-12 teams recruiting me. Then I had the two knee injuries and a lot of it disappeared. I was very lucky that Princeton still wanted me and, being honest, it couldn't have worked out better.

"Being honest, Princeton—the college—was a backup plan. It took me four years to get back to a place where I think I have a chance. Don't get me wrong, I'm really happy to be leaving with a Princeton degree.

"But my goal was always to get to the NFL. It's still my goal."

Nicholas was one of those kids who had been pushed very hard at a young age by his father. "He was brutal," Nicholas said, laughing. "He was one of those dads who was never satisfied. I could have three interceptions in a game and he'd get on me about not getting a fourth. My personality is a lot like his, so we had some real shouting matches. But when I got hurt and wondered if I'd play football again, he could not have been more supportive. He kept telling me that one way or another everything would turn out all right. It made us much closer."

Nicholas's co-captain and fellow linebacker Liam Johnson had been the Ivy League Defensive Player of the Year in 2022. Johnson had grown up in the Philadelphia suburb of Moorestown, New Jersey, and had two brothers and a cousin who had played at Princeton.

While Nicholas decided against returning to the West Coast as a grad transfer, Johnson went west, transferring to Cal-Berkeley. What was most fascinating about the transfers was the quality of football played at the schools recruiting them.

"You're not just talking about FBS schools, you're talking about big-time FBS schools, ones that might very easily lead to the NFL or at the very least a shot at the NFL," Bob Surace said. "I think that's evidence of the quality of football we play and it's also evidence of how well they're coached in the Ivy League."

Two Ivy League players were drafted by NFL teams in the 2024 draft—both from Yale. Kiran Amegadjie, a six-foot-five, 326-pound offensive tackle, was taken in the third round by the Chicago Bears, a very high pick for an Ivy League school. Nick Gargiulo, also an offensive lineman, was taken in the seventh round by the Denver Broncos after starting all twelve games in 2023 as a graduate transfer at South Carolina and being named All-SEC.

The quality of Ivy League players was easy to see before almost every Ivy League game when NFL scouts—usually at least a half dozen of them—came down to the sidelines to say hello to the coaches. An hour before Princeton played Harvard, the scouts engulfed Surace wanting to know if Jalen Travis was going to play.

He had hoped to return to the lineup that day, but when he went out to warm up, he could tell his knee wasn't quite ready for a game.

"You all want to know about 71 [Travis]?" Surace asked. "He tried—believe me, he wanted to play, but he's just not ready to go. It'll be next week."

The scouts were disappointed but understood. "And anyway," one of them said, "they've got a couple guys on defense worth looking at too."

It's different with college coaches, who are a bit too busy on Saturdays to scout in person. Plus, very few colleges have the budget to travel assistants to other games. Instead, they look at a good deal of tape on players and talk to one another about players they've seen.

Ivy League players are often in demand, not just because they're good football players but because of what else they bring with them. Almost without fail, they're college graduates with no academic issues. If they choose to seriously pursue a master's degree, that's a bonus, but if they just go through the motions for a semester while they are playing football, that's fine too. Also almost without fail, they are good "character" kids.

"Coaches know they're good kids; they aren't going to be a headache in any way," Reno said. "It's the same with the NFL. You get a kid like that on your roster, even if he's not a star, he's bound to be a good guy in the locker room."

The reason Ivy League players are often overlooked coming out of high school by FBS programs is usually size, sometimes speed, and sometimes both. Given a choice, many would go to an FBS school because they grow up dreaming about playing for Alabama or Michigan or Clemson or Georgia.

If Penn quarterback Aidan Sayin's younger brother Jordan—the one recruited by multiple FBS schools who chose Alabama, but then transferred to Ohio State when Nick Saban retired—had decided to go to Penn, he could have spent a year backing up his big brother and then succeeded him. Jordan wanted the big time.

The most intriguing quarterback situation in the league going into 2024 was at Harvard. Charles DePrima had been brilliant the first half of the season, arguably the conference Player of the Year in leading Harvard to a 5–0 start.

But the Princeton defense made his life miserable, and he was never quite the same after that game. "We ruined his season," said Princeton linebacker Ozzie Nicholas—never one to hold back in his opinion. "He was great before our game. Not so much from our game forward."

A week later, against Dartmouth, Murphy split time between DePrima and Jaden Craig, the sophomore he thought had huge talent. A week after that, at Columbia, Murphy decided to start Craig and DePrima became the forgotten man in the quarterback room.

"It was a very tough decision," Murphy said, "especially since Charles had played so well in the first five games. We were divided as a staff. In the end, we felt as if Jaden was on an upswing and Charles wasn't. Plus, we were confident that Charles would handle it well, wouldn't sulk.

"When I called him in to tell him what we were doing, you could tell he wasn't happy—who would be?—but as I expected, he never sulked or pouted."

Craig played well in the easy (38–24) win over Columbia and was the receiver on the winning "Crimson Special" play in the third overtime against Penn. He wasn't as good against a very good Yale defense, but there was no doubt in Murphy's mind that he would be Harvard's quarterback for the next two seasons.

"He has a chance to be the best quarterback we've had here since Ryan Fitzpatrick," Murphy said. "He's got everything you need to be great. He's smart, he's fast, and he's got a cannon for an arm."

Fitzpatrick, who graduated in 2005, had led Harvard to a 10–0 record as a senior and had been the 250th pick—out of 258—in the 2005 NFL draft. He ended up playing for nine teams over seventeen seasons. Often, he was signed as a backup but ended up as a starter. Late in his career, he became the Miami Dolphins' starter and played so well he earned the nickname "FitzMagic."

Even when a serious ankle injury forced him to retire in 2022, he was still doing TV commercials as FitzMagic.

To be put into the same sentence as FitzMagic by the man who coached him in college was elite company. And Murphy was never a man given to hyperbole.

Because almost no one transfers from Harvard—especially a year away from a degree—DePrima returned to Harvard for his senior year.

That meant the Crimson would have two quarterbacks with experience and a new coach in 2024. It would certainly make for a fascinating fall in Cambridge—and, across the river, in Boston.

# Chapter Fourteen

ROBIN HARRIS HAS HAD THE title of "executive director of the Ivy League Council of Presidents" for fifteen years. In non–Ivy League English, that means she's the league's commissioner.

With all due respect to Ms. Harris, who has done fine work in a job often weighed down by Ivy League snobbery—much of it from the presidents; a good deal of it from alumni and faculty—the best known nonplayer or coach connected to the league is Jack Ford.

By a wide margin. He is, unofficially, the league's mayor. Of course, if the presidents ever gave him an official title, it would probably be something like "Lord Mayor and liaison from the outside world to all league supplicants."

Naturally, not only would Ford not want any sort of title but he would laugh at the notion that he deserves any sort of title.

"I'm just very lucky to get to do what I get to do with the league," he said. "It's fun, I like to think we're doing a good job, and I get paid to do it. Are you kidding me? Not only would I do it for nothing, I'd probably pay *them* to do it."

Ford graduated from Yale in 1972 and would be the first to admit his Yale bias. "My partner [Eric Frede] can tell you there are moments during a Yale game where I'll shake my fist after a big play," he said. "But I try to keep it out of my voice at all times."

He has succeeded superbly since taking over as the analyst for the Ivy League's package of games on ESPN in 2018.

"When I first heard that Jack was going to be the analyst, I was a little concerned because he was a Yale grad," former Harvard coach Tim Murphy said. "The rivalries, especially Harvard-Yale, are pretty intense. But as time went on, I realized he was simply terrific at what he did: smart, prepared, and I never once felt any bias. I'm not saying it wasn't there, just that I never felt it when I watched him doing any game, including Harvard-Yale."

"Tim told me that a few years ago," Ford said. "It was one of the nicest compliments I've ever gotten."

Ford was raised in Point Pleasant, New Jersey, by a single mother. He was a very good student but would be the first one to tell you it was football that got him into Yale. Freshmen weren't eligible when Ford arrived at Yale in 1968, but he was a starting linebacker in 1969 on a team that stunned the league by tying with Princeton and Dartmouth for the title coming off the disastrous ("Harvard beats Yale 29–29,") end to the 1968 season.

Ford had a 77-yard interception return for a touchdown against Penn as a sophomore and was a solid three-year starter for the Bulldogs. When he graduated in 1972, he was accepted into Fordham law school. He was able to pay his way through law school thanks to three winning appearances on *Jeopardy*, and he went to work after graduation as a prosecutor in New Jersey.

In 1984, WCBS-TV in New York hired him as a legal correspondent, which led to a remarkably varied TV career during which he has worked for all three national networks. He first gained national notoriety when he covered all nine months of the O.J. Simpson trial for Court TV, where he had begun to work when it was launched in 1991.

He worked as a legal correspondent and was also an anchor on *Weekend Today* and other network shows. He even hosted ESPN's *The Sports Reporters* for two years, the network leaning into his days as an Ivy League football player.

Nowadays, he works for CBS and teaches a class at Yale called "Famous Courtroom Trials"—a job he's held for seventeen years. He is writing his second book; the first was a thriller, but this is a real-life story about a female World War II correspondent.

He's in constant demand as a speaker and returns to his first love every fall: Ivy League football.

"I love the people in the league. I really enjoy the coaches and the players. I enjoy the research I do before every game and being at the games," he said. "It's always fun and it's almost always competitive. Most of the games in this league are close. This year [2023] was wild in so many ways." He paused and laughed. "I think I say that at the end of every season."

Like everyone else in the league, Ford was amazed by Dartmouth's story. "The fact that they rebounded from losing Buddy was nothing short of amazing—or maybe more than that," he said. "If I believed in the strange powers of the afterlife, that would have been something to seriously think about. I don't think anyone thought they could rebound from the tragedies they suffered and somehow become a serious contender. And yet, that's exactly what they did."

Although, as Murphy points out, it is difficult to tell that Ford is a graduate of one of the eight schools—much less a former player—during broadcasts, he readily admits there are moments in the booth when he has to remind himself that he's there as a commentator and not as a fan.

"If I told you I don't shake my fist on occasion or get excited when Yale makes a big play, I'd be lying to you," he said. "But I always remind myself that I have to keep my voice under control. Describe the play I just saw, talk about what may come next. Of course it's harder to do in Yale-Harvard, but I think, through the years, I've done a pretty good job controlling or at least concealing my emotions."

Ford readily admits that the last play of the 2023 The Game almost got to him when Jaden Craig's final pass of the day missed Cooper Barkate in the end zone by inches. "I think I almost stopped breathing during the play," he said. "When it went over his fingertips, I did a double fist pump. Then I got hold of myself and explained the replay. It was so close."

Having three new coaches in 2024 would be something different for Ford since the league's head coaches had been so stable for so many years.

"Part of it is that the Ivy League tends to give coaches a longer leash than other leagues do. You look back on Buddy Teevens and Tim Murphy, Tony Reno and Bob Surace from this generation. All became very successful but only after struggling for several seasons."

The best example was Teevens, who was 9–41 during the first five seasons of his second stint at Dartmouth—including a 0–10 record in his fourth season—but kept his job and undoubtedly would have retired of his own volition if not for his premature death.

Archer was given ten years by Cornell. Only two of Cornell's last ten coaches dating to 1975 left with winning records. But Archer readily admitted that 29–71 wasn't good enough, even at a job that is always going to be difficult for any coach.

Fabish only had one season as interim coach after Al Bagnoli retired for health reasons six weeks before the season began, but Bagnoli coached seven teams at Columbia and, after going 2–8 and 3–7 his first two seasons, he went 30–20 the next five, including 8–2 and 7–3 in two of those seasons—numbers unheard of at Columbia.

"I'm not sure people understand what an extraordinary job Al did at Columbia," Ford said. "Realistically, any time Columbia goes 5–5, they should be happy. It's a really tough job; location, just having get to and from practice every day, their tradition of losing. He broke through all that."

Bagnoli's classic quote about the difference between Columbia and Penn, where he won nine Ivy League titles in twenty-three seasons, sums it up quite well: "At Penn, if we lost two in a row, people would say, 'Maybe it's time for the old coach to hang it up.' Here [Columbia] when we won two in a row, they wanted to build a statue to me."

Fabish would probably have to have gone at *least* 5–5, maybe 6–4, to have a serious chance to be retained. And, while he believed his team had played better than its record (it had), he had no bitterness when he wasn't retained. "It was a great experience, both as an assistant and as coach," he said. "I'm grateful for that. I wish I'd had more time—I thought we [he and his staff] deserved more time—but that's the way coaching is."

Or, as Hyman Roth once said to Michael Corleone, "This is the business we've chosen."

While Ford felt badly for Fabish and Archer, the coaching change that hit him hardest was Tim Murphy's decision to retire.

"I understand the decision completely," he said. "Very few coaches get to walk away while they're still on top. Tim was able to do that and I'm very happy for him. He'd gone a few years without a league title [2015], and his team played very well all season to finish tied for the title, and they were a few inches away from winning it outright.

"I remember, toward the end of his career, my coach, Carm Cozza, was getting questions all the time about how much longer he was going to coach, and it clearly affected recruiting and hurt the program. I'm glad that never happened to Murph."

Cozza was sixty-six when he retired after losing records in four of his last five seasons. Harvard's tie for first place in 2023 allowed Murphy to match Cozza with ten Ivy League titles. Cozza won his last championship in 1989 and then coached seven more seasons. Murphy opted to coach no more seasons after his last title, although he was a year older than Cozza when he stepped down.

"I understand Tim's decision, I really do," Ford said. "I think winning the title definitely helped him make the decision, but I also know Buddy's death weighed on him all season. I think it made it difficult for him to enjoy coaching even though his team performed so well.

"I've heard nothing but good things about Coach [Andrew] Aurich, but there definitely has to be a void in the league with [Murphy] gone. He had so much success in what isn't an easy job, and he always did it the right way. You could always count on meeting exceptional kids when you were at Harvard, and they had very good players.

"For me, knowing nothing about what comes next there, it's very sad that he's gone.

"The amount of change in the coaching ranks in the last year has been remarkable. You had one tragedy, two firings, and Tim being able to walk away on his own terms. I'm happy for Tim, but, like I said, I'm sad for the rest of the league."

In all, there were four coaches who were not in place at the beginning of 2023 in charge on the sidelines when the 2024 season began. For a league that prides itself on stability, that borders on shocking.

"I guess it's fair to say that nothing's really surprising in this league anymore," Ford said. "We'd had two seasons in sixty-five in which two-loss teams tied for the title [1963 and 1982]. Then last year we had three teams tie with two losses. Yale and Harvard at the top of the league is no surprise and I know Dartmouth had won twenty championships, but under last year's circumstances, no way anyone picked them to win a title.

"Crazy year. But then again, one of the things about the Ivy League that's fun is that just about every year is crazy. Two years ago, four teams had a chance to win or tie for the title going into the last week. This past year, *five* teams were still in contention going into the second to last week. And two teams were eliminated that day; both lost in overtime. You never really know what's coming next."

About the only thing the Ivy League can be certain of is that, when the season starts, the Mayor will be ready to go.

Again, there is no trophy given to the winner of The Game, just the game ball, which ends up in the hands of the head coach and, once the team is in the locker room, in the hands of the team captain.

"It's my most cherished possession," said Wande Owens, Yale's 2023 captain. I'm sitting here looking at it right now and getting chills all over again remembering Coach [Tony Reno] handing it to me."

Owens was sitting in his room at the University of New Hampshire as he spoke. He had graduated from Yale in December and had graduate-transferred to UNH in January. New Hampshire had finished its season on the same day of The Game by beating Maine in the Battle for the Brice-Cowell Musket. The antique musket, donated by alumni of both schools, features a forty-three-inch barrel and rests in a wood case.

"I'll happily take the game ball," Owens said with a laugh.

Owens and the rest of the Yale seniors were able to walk away from their final season at Yale with a feeling of accomplishment after going 3–3 in their first six games.

"I think we were just trying too hard to be a great team," Owens said. "It had been a long time since Yale had won the league two years in a row [three straight from 1979 to 1981] and we wanted to be special. We had key players back and we had most of the leadership from the previous year back. But we put a lot of pressure on ourselves because of that instead of feeling confident because of it. We were overwhelming favorites to win again. I think that got to us, got inside our heads.

"I lost a lot of sleep trying to figure out where we had gone wrong, where *I* had gone wrong. I felt like as the captain, I was failing."

"The Cornell game [week two] stunned us. Then, in the Penn game [week six], we got punched in the mouth. The next day we had a team meeting to try to figure out what was going on. I was miserable because I was the captain and I felt responsible for the fact that we'd gotten punched in the mouth and hadn't been able to respond.

"It was [linebacker] Hamilton Moore and [offensive tackle] Sean Sullivan who came up with the idea that we have to approach the rest of the season as if there's blood on the water. We came up with a saying, 'Don't let the boys win one. Or two. Or three.' That kind of became our mantra the rest of the season."

Important as that meeting might have been, Owens believes a senior get-together a week later after a dominant win over Columbia might have been even more important.

"We hadn't really meshed as a senior class for a variety of reasons," Owens said. "I lost all sorts of sleep trying to figure out what was wrong, what I could do as the captain to get us turned around.

"But that night, we all went out just for fun. We were relaxed because we'd won easily that day. We went to a karaoke bar and we all sang. I sang 'Lovely Day' by Bill Withers. I wasn't very good but neither was anyone else. That wasn't the point though. After that night, I think we felt closer as a senior class and it had an effect on the whole team."

On the morning of the Columbia game, Tony Reno sat in the trailer serving as his office during the locker room renovation and talked about his players' approach to the last four games of the season.

"We lost to Penn [handily] because they were good, maybe the best they've been all season, and we were bad, maybe the worst we've been all season. The outcome was exactly what it should have been.

"Look, injuries can always be an excuse. Every team has them, but we've had *a lot* so far. We can very easily use that as an excuse and pack it in from here. I've told the guys that. I also told them I think they are capable of winning the last four games we have left even with our injuries. I also told them that, depending on our attitude, we could lose all four games. I don't think there's a team we can't beat left or a team we can't lose to."

If there was a team that might look like a walkover on Yale's schedule, it would be Columbia. The Lions were 0–3 in the league at that moment, but two of the losses had come very late in games they had led into the fourth quarter. Their defense was ranked number one in the *country* and the Bulldogs were expecting a difficult game.

"When we watched their defense on film that week, we expected a tough time," quarterback Nolan Grooms said. "They really played hard and they hit hard. That's what we expected."

Grooms had been the Ivy League Offensive Player of the Year as a junior. Like his team, he had been up and down for the first six games of the season.

"I don't know what it is, but I seem to play my best only after I feel like I have my back against the wall," he said. "I was that way in high school and I've been that way a lot in college. Can't really explain it."

Grooms had grown up in Lake Wylie, South Carolina, the son of James and Sharon Grooms. His dad was a high school football coach, which Nolan thinks played a big role in making him the player he became, even though he never played for his father.

"I was on the sideline on Friday nights growing up. I think that helped with my understanding of the game but also had something to do with how intense I became on the field because I was always up close to what was going on and knew what a difference it made if you really got after it or didn't get after it."

He laughed. "I've spent a lot of Sundays apologizing to teammates for things I said on Saturday during a game. I thank God that Wande was the captain because he had a kind of cool that I just don't have."

Grooms started to get interest from colleges during his junior year. Among them were Virginia and Florida State. But his first offer came from Yale, where he had gone to summer camp on a couple of occasions. He was still undecided during his senior season when his father got a call from Tyler Whitley, who was the coach at the Taft School, an elite academic boarding school in Watertown, Connecticut, about thirty miles north of New Haven.

"Dad had sent a kid—Joe Smith—to Taft for a year of post-graduate football. He'd done well there and Coach Whitley thought it would be a good thing for me too. So, I went up there.

"At that point, to be honest, I'd been going to get an offer from one of the FBS schools that had been in touch with me. I finally realized that the FBS schools were waiting to see who dropped off their board before offering guys like me either a scholarship or a preferred walk-on spot.

"I was holding Yale off because of that. After a while though, it occurred to me that I was at a school with six hundred great students and just about all of them would be thrilled to go to Yale. I woke up one morning and said, 'Why wouldn't you want to go to Yale? Good football, great academics, what was I waiting for?'

"Right after that, I committed."

Little did he know that it would be more than two years before he would get a serious chance to play again. He threw five passes (all complete) as a freshman, but his entire sophomore season was wiped out by the Ivy League's decision to cancel all sports in the fall of 2020.

Even though the pandemic meant no football in 2020 and one semester taking classes remotely, he enjoyed Yale. "I did hear a good bit about my southern accent when I was a freshman," he said with a laugh. "I don't think it's as noticeable now as it was then, but when I go home, I slip right back into it."

A lefty with a southern accent at Yale—not your prototypical Ivy League quarterback.

He finally got his chance to play in 2021 when Reno made a quarterback change with his team trailing U-Conn 17–0 at halftime in the fifth game of the season. Grooms almost rallied his team to a win in that game, Yale finally losing, 21–15. The Bulldogs won their next three games (including a 63–38 win at Brown) before losing to Princeton and then to Harvard, 34–31 when the Crimson drove 66 yards in fifty-nine seconds—with no time-outs left—for the winning touchdown.

A year later, Grooms was clearly established as Yale's quarterback from start to finish, and when the Bulldogs finished 6–1 in the league and won the conference title outright, he was chosen as the Asa S. Bushnell Offensive Player of the Year. (Asa S. Bushnell was a Princeton graduate who was the school's athletic director and commissioner of the then-important Eastern College Athletic Conference for thirty-two years.)

Grooms beat out Harvard running back Aidan Borguet for the award. Borguet had rushed for 1,183 yards in ten games, but Grooms got the nod from the eight Ivy League coaches who choose the winner.

"I think I won it because we won the league outright," he said. "Otherwise, you could see why they might have given it to Borguet."

Jack Ford is a believer that the key to success in the Ivy League—even more than in other conferences—is having a good quarterback. "Look at Harvard," he said. "When they were dominating the league, they seemed to have the best quarterback every year. When Grooms became Yale's quarterback, they won the league in back-to-back years. It wasn't a coincidence."

Grooms took a lot of the blame for Yale's poor start in 2023. He struggled and so did his team. "I think it was a combination of things," he said. "We put all sorts of pressure on ourselves to win two in a row and none of us handled it very well. And we *did* have a lot of injuries. That's not excuse-making, that's just a fact."

Going into the Columbia game, Yale had eleven players standing on the sidelines on crutches, most of them starters. Watching them go down the tunnel—first stairs, then downhill—to the field was almost painful to watch.

The low point had come in the loss to Penn in the season's sixth week. "When we came off the field that day, we figured we were done," Grooms said. "No one wins the Ivy League with two conference losses. Then we heard that Princeton had beaten Harvard and all of a sudden we weren't done."

Princeton's victory over then-unbeaten Harvard suddenly made it a wide-open race. Harvard and Princeton each had one loss while Yale, Dartmouth, Penn, and Cornell each had only two losses.

"We knew after Princeton won that the season wasn't over for us," Wande Owens said. "We had absolutely no margin for error, we'd used that up. But there was still a chance. It was still in our hands. No excuses, just don't let the boys win one. And I mean *one*."

Four games, four wins. And an improbable ending to an improbable season.

# Chapter Fifteen

It didn't take very long for Columbia and Cornell to target their new coaches. One might suspect that the athletic directors—Peter Pilling at Columbia and Nicki Moore at Cornell—had already targeted their next coaches even before the season was over.

It is an interesting sidenote that five of the Ivy League's eight athletic directors are women. That number—62.5 percent of the league—stacks up very well when compared with the national average off 21.8 percent of Division I athletic directors—FBS and FCS—being women.

Additionally, Robin Harris, the Ivy League's executive director/commissioner, has been on the job since 2009. The league's staff consists of twelve people and the office is about two miles from Princeton Stadium, at the edge of the Princeton campus.

On the flip side of that show of progress and diversity, there are no Black football head coaches in the league right now. In fact, the Ivy League has only had two Black head football coaches in history: Columbia's Norries Wilson, who had a record of 17–43 from 2006 to 2011, and Yale's Tom Williams, who went 16–14 from 2009 to

2011 before being forced to resign under a cloud after it came out that he had not, as he had claimed, been a Rhodes Scholar candidate while at Stanford.

Dan Swanstrom grew up in Houston and went to Division 3 Rhodes College in Memphis where he was twice a D-3 All-American at quarterback. He played overseas, in Germany, for a year before coming home to Houston to become an assistant coach at Stratford High School where he coached future No. 1 NFL draft pick Andrew Luck. He moved up to the college ranks at Redlands College in southern California and from there to Johns Hopkins and then to his first stint at Penn.

Nicki Moore didn't know Swanstrom, but she knew of him. He had been the head coach at Ithaca College—which is less than two miles from Cornell—from 2017 to 2021. Swanstrom had left Ithaca with a 32–11 record (and three D-3 conference titles) to go back to Penn. He had previously been there as the quarterbacks coach from 2014 to 2016, hired by Al Bagnoli.

When Bagnoli's successor, Ray Priore, asked him to come back to the school as offensive coordinator, he decided to take the risk of going from a program where "I could have coached for life" to an Ivy League school that was coming off a rare (3–7) down season.

"If I stay at Ithaca, I know I'm never going to get fired," he said. "That's reassuring when you have [three] young children. I knew how good a coach and man Ray was because I had worked with him my first time around. But I also know that sports is about winning and if we had another bad season, who knows what might have happened?"

In the end, Swanstrom went back to Penn. He loved coaching in the Ivy League—and he loved the idea of coaching in the Ivy League.

"My main recruiting area had been Texas," he said. "I remember there was a camp that had a bunch of kids in it who were potential Ivy League players. There were at least six assistants from Ivies, including me, down there to scout. One night, we all just went to dinner together. I remember sitting there while we were swapping stories thinking, 'This doesn't happen in any other league.' It wasn't as if we weren't competing, but there's a bond when you coach in the Ivy League. I always liked that."

In 2022, Swanstrom's first season back at Penn, the Quakers finished 5–2 (one game behind Yale for the league title) and 8–2 overall. A year later, after losing two games in overtime and one other in the final minutes, they finished 6–4 and a disappointing 3–4 in conference play.

"A lot of it was just inexperience," he said. "We had two converted quarterbacks at wide receiver, and they were learning on the job. They literally had to learn how to properly catch the ball. We also had four sophomores and a freshman on the offensive line. They kept getting better, but we lost two games because of fumbles on the snap.

"Don't get me wrong, they're good players, who will be much better next season. And, we had a terrific quarterback [Aidan Sayin] who often held us together. We still averaged over 400 yards a game on offense. I think next season, their offense will be great."

Swanstrom's first contact with Cornell came the Monday after Thanksgiving, nine days after the season ended. These days, first contact for almost any college job is from a headhunter. Exactly why ADs need a headhunter no one really knows, but it has become a booming business in the last twenty-five years.

Swanstrom told the headhunter he would be interested in the job. During the next week, he had several conversations with athletic director Nicki Moore, who invited him to campus for a face-to-face interview on Monday, December 3.

"I decided before I went up there that if I was offered the job, I was taking it. I wasn't going to negotiate, do the used-car salesman bit. If they wanted me, I wanted them. I knew the school, I knew the area, and I knew the kind of kids you coach in the Ivy League."

Moore offered him the job the next day. On December 5, the school announced that he would be the twenty-eighth head football coach in school history. "I pretty much accepted on the spot," he said. "I was thrilled when Nicki made the offer, and I was ready to go."

Swanstrom is well aware of Cornell's recent history, but says he is undaunted by it. "I really believe I was put on this earth to do one thing—and that's be a college football head coach," he said. "I've thought that since I was a player and then as an assistant coach.

"Every place I've been [John Hopkins, Penn, Ithaca, and Penn again], we've had success. It isn't as if Cornell doesn't have history, it just isn't recent history. I know how hard Dave Archer worked and I think he's a very good football coach. I know him from my days at Ithaca when we were frequently at events together.

"I didn't do any research or preparation before I formally interviewed for this job, I just went in and told them who I was, what I wanted to do, and why I thought I'd be a good coach for Cornell. I know the things we have to overcome, but I wouldn't be here if I didn't believe I could get it done."

At his first meeting with his new players, Swanstrom's opening statement was direct: "You didn't choose me, I chose you."

"I was trying to make the point to them that I knew them, I'd competed against them, and I'd seen the program up close when I was at Ithaca and I believed the talent in the room was good enough to compete in the Ivy League," he said. "I know the league;

I scouted every team's defense for the last two years, so I wasn't just spewing hyperbole. I meant what I said."

Swanstrom also had the advantage going into his first season with a talented, experienced quarterback in Jameson Wang.

"I knew Jameson was talented before I got here," he said. "Now that I've seen him up close, he's better than I thought. He's not only athletically gifted, but he has a very high football IQ. Our offense is designed for his kind of game."

Wang was probably as close to Archer as anyone on the team. Even though the team never formally met after Archer's firing, Wang called his former coach right away. "I wanted to thank him for everything he'd done for me," Wang said. "If it weren't for him, I wouldn't be at Cornell, and going to Cornell is the best thing I've ever done.

"I think we were all caught a little off guard when we got the email Saturday night saying there was a Zoom meeting with the athletic director on Sunday. I know I hadn't been focused on Coach Archer's job status. But as soon as I saw the email, I guessed what it was about."

Wang was unaware at the time that Archer had been told before the Columbia game that he was going to be fired. When he heard, he was unhappy. "I just don't think that's the way to do things," he said. "You don't tell a coach he's being fired when he still has a game or games to coach. It just isn't the right way to do things." He paused for a second and added, "And you can quote me on that."

One other thing certain to help Swanstrom is a $54 million indoor facility—for all sports—that is scheduled to break ground early in 2025. "They've raised $48 million so far," Swanstrom said. "They decided not to start until they had 100 percent of the money. It will definitely help us."

For all the talk from Cornell players and coaches about the lack of an indoor facility being a symbol of the school's blue collar football image, there's no doubt having a year-round indoor practice field will help the program—especially during the offseason winter months when snow and extreme cold are often a part of daily life in Ithaca.

"So far, I've really liked everything Coach Swan has done—on and off the practice field. It doesn't change the way I feel about Coach Archer," said Wang, "but I think they made the right decision on his successor."

It took Cornell seventeen days to find a new coach. Columbia found its successor to Mark Fabish three days earlier than that. Jon Poppe had graduated from Williams in 2007—the Ephs went 8–0 during his senior season—and he had been an assistant coach at both Harvard and Columbia, working for Tim Murphy and for Al Bagnoli.

He'd become the head coach at D-3 Union College in upstate New York in 2023 and had gone 10–2 in his one season there. Columbia AD Peter Pilling had his eye on Poppe throughout that fall and Poppe got the job three weeks before turning forty.

Knowing that Columbia's weakness in 2023 had been at quarterback, Poppe took the unusual [for the Ivy League] step of seeking a transfer quarterback and got one—Northwestern's Cole Freeman. Even though he didn't play often at Northwestern, the fact that Freeman was recruited by a Big Ten school would indicate that he will be an upgrade for the Lions.

With a similar outlook as Swanstrom, Poppe believes Columbia isn't that far from at least returning to the levels that Al Bagnoli reached in his eight years in charge.

"Coach Bagnoli proved that Columbia *can* be successful, it's just not easy. I knew that from my time here and was certainly aware of it when I was first contacted about the job," he said. "I also know that if you *do* have success here, people at Columbia will notice. I was here his first three years and watched him do it, so I have an understanding of what it takes.

"We [my family] had a great time at Union, but an Ivy League job was impossible to turn down. Plus, I know the school, I know the city, and I know the league. All those things will definitely help."

Columbia's 3–7 record in 2023 was only its second losing season in six. So while the Lions' 2023 record made it easier for AD Peter Pilling to make the decision to change coaches, it was also deceiving given the close games Columbia lost.

"Winning is what you're judged on," Mark Fabish said. "Coaches know that, and players do too. Before I met with Peter, I put together a memo on all the things we'd done well during the season, especially given the circumstances. We only won one league game—Harvard and Yale were better than us, but we could have won any of the other four games we lost. We split those games and finish 5–5 and who knows what might have happened?"

It didn't take long for Fabish to find work: In March he was hired as the new coach at The Peddie School, a prestigious private school in Hightstown, New Jersey—about seventy miles south of where Fabish had grown up, played, and coached in Bergen County. Peddie had finished 2–7 in 2023, so Fabish wouldn't have to worry about his record in 2024—especially without the word "interim" tag as part of his title.

"It's nice to start with a clean slate," Fabish said. "I will always be grateful for the opportunity I was given by Columbia. No hard feelings at all, just some disappointment. I've coached in high school before, so I think I know what it's about. I'm looking forward to it."

---

The most-watched new coach in the Ivy League would undoubtedly be Harvard's new coach, Andrew Aurich. The new coach—regardless of who it was—would be under intense scrutiny. Although Aurich was only thirty-nine, he had a lengthy and varied résumé as an assistant coach, first at the high school level, then at the D-3 level, followed by eight years at his alma mater, Princeton, a brief stint in the NFL in Tampa Bay, and then four years coaching down the road at Rutgers.

Most people had expected Murphy's successor to be one of his coordinators—Mickey Fein on offense or Scott Larkee on defense. Larkee appeared to be the front-runner, largely because he had a Harvard degree (1999), had played for Murphy, and had been on Murphy's staff for the previous sixteen years. Fein had been at Harvard for eight years. He had graduated from Maine in 1999 and had coached at Lafayette for nine seasons before coming to Harvard.

The hiring was controversial enough that athletic director Erin McDermott admitted that a number of boosters had told her they would withdraw their financial support and that there had been backlash from former players—including many of the 2023 seniors.

She denied that there had been a lack of transparency from the committee that had ultimately recommended Aurich over the internal candidates. Three former Harvard players, Eion Hu, Andrew Berry, and Ryan Fitzpatrick, led the search committee; Fitzpatrick the most famous of the group after seventeen seasons in the NFL.

Aurich knew about the criticism of the choice and said—like any new head coach—that developing relationships would be the key to his being successful.

The real key to success, however, would be winning games. This was where Aurich would face a different challenge than other first-year Ivy coaches. The eight men who began the calendar year in

2023 as Ivy football coaches had a combined record in their first two seasons in charge of their teams of 49–111.

Some continued to lose and then turned it around. Buddy Teevens had five straight losing seasons in his second stint at Dartmouth, beginning in 2005, including going 0–10 in 2008, his fourth season. The school remained patient, perhaps because he had been a star quarterback in the 1970s or because he had turned it around during his first stint in the 1980s.

Regardless, it worked out well. Dartmouth didn't have a losing season during the next eleven years, including going 9–1 four times. Bob Surace was 2–18 in his first two seasons at Princeton. Since then, he has twice gone 5–5, gone 10–0 once, and has had winning seasons every year since 2013.

For others, it hasn't worked out so well. Dave Archer's best record in ten years at Cornell was 5–5.

The most analogous situation to Aurich was Penn coach Ray Priore, who had succeeded the hugely successful Al Bagnoli in 2015. Bagnoli had won nine Ivy League titles in twenty-three seasons at Penn, but back-to-back losing seasons had led to the decision that he step down to become an administrator. The office job had ended three months later when Peter Pilling had offered him the Columbia coaching job.

"I realized I wasn't ready to give up coaching," Bagnoli said. "I told Pete what I needed to have a chance to be competitive and he said yes to all of them. So, I took it."

In the fifty-nine Ivy League seasons prior to Bagnoli's arrival, Columbia had four winning seasons. In Bagnoli's seven seasons, Columbia had four winning seasons, including four of the last five. That would explain why he was inducted into the Columbia Hall of Fame about fifteen minutes after he retired on a rainy October afternoon when Columbia hosted Penn, Bagnoli's former team. Remember his line about Columbia building him a statue after two straight wins? The statue may be coming soon.

As Bagnoli walked off the field at the end of the time-out where his Hall of Fame induction had been announced, Mark Fabish took off his headset and raced over to congratulate his former coach and boss.

Priore had already been at Penn as an assistant coach for twenty-eight years when he succeeded Bagnoli. He had been at the school for five years when Bagnoli took over. He knew the league and he knew the school when he took over in 2015. The Quakers were 7–3 in his first two seasons and won back-to-back Ivy League titles. They were 6–4 in 2023, including the triple-overtime loss to Harvard. A win in that game and they would have played Princeton the final week with a chance to tie for another title.

Aurich took over a team that had tied for first in the Ivy League and had two talented quarterbacks returning: junior Jaden Craig and senior Charles DePrima. Both had shown flashes of brilliance in 2023—DePrima in the first half of the season and Craig in the last four games.

Because of his speed (sub-4.5 in the 40), DePrima would start the 2024 season as a slash: wide receiver/quarterback. A year earlier, Harvard began the season with no experience at quarterback. In 2024, the Crimson would have two quarterbacks who had performed well against Ivy League teams.

At most schools, a player—especially a quarterback—who lost his job at midseason would have been in the transfer portal about five minutes—or less—after it opened. DePrima wasn't going anywhere: players don't transfer when they are one year from an Ivy League degree.

Aurich's first truly important move was to retain most of Murphy's staff, including Larkee and Fein. He met with the players less than three weeks after getting the job to tell them that he had asked most of the staff to return. The move wasn't formally announced for another month, but the players were pleased with the news, and it seemed to bring an end—or at least a pause—to the bickering that had come with Aurich's hiring.

Of course how Aurich would be judged wouldn't really begin until September 21—when Harvard would open its season at Harvard Stadium hosting Stetson. The Crimson's first two Ivy League games would be on the road: at Brown and at Cornell.

Harvard and Yale will no doubt be picked 1–2 in the preseason media poll. To say that Aurich will face high expectations is a vast understatement. Welcome back to the Ivy League, Coach.

# Epilogue

When I first made the decision to write *The Ancient Eight*, I felt confident I would find a number of great stories to tell and would enjoy most of the players I interviewed.

I was wrong.

I interviewed eighty-two players from the eight teams and *all* eighty-two had stories to tell and told them with patience, humor, and honesty. A lot of them wanted to keep playing for one more year as graduate transfers. They were highly recruited by FBS schools for two basic reasons: they all had their undergraduate degrees and—more important to the big-time schools—they could play.

Some had (and have) hopes to play in the National Football League, which isn't unreasonable given that twelve former Ivy League players were on NFL teams in 2022 and 2023 and three more were taken in the 2024 NFL draft, including Yale offensive tackle Kiran Amegadjie, who went to the Chicago Bears in the third round with the seventy-fifth pick in the draft. Center Hunter Nourzad, who had graduated from Cornell in 2022 and grad-transferred to Penn State, was taken in the fifth round by the Super

Bowl champion Kansas City Chiefs. Nick Gargiulo, who had been Yale's captain in 2022 and had spent a grad transfer season at South Carolina, was taken in the seventh round by the Denver Broncos.

Gargiulo was the 256th player chosen, meaning he missed being "Mr. Irrelevant"—the last player selected—by one spot. It's worth noting that Mr. Irrelevant 2021 was quarterback Brock Purdy, who led the San Francisco 49ers to the Super Bowl in February of 2024. Alabama safety Jaylen Key was Mr. Irrelevant, going one spot after Gargiulo.

The best known seventh-round draft pick from the Ivy League was Ryan Fitzpatrick, who went 250th out of 258 selections in 2005 and played in the NFL for seventeen seasons, about half of them as a starter. He played for nine teams and started at some point for all nine. The only team he didn't throw a touchdown pass for was Washington, which signed him to start in 2021. He suffered a season-ending hip injury in the team's opener and retired the next summer a few months shy of forty.

I knew the Ivy League was respected when I started my research, but I was surprised when I saw the number of scouts who showed up to watch Ivy League players week in and week out. The largest group had come to watch offensive tackle Jalen Travis's return from injury against Harvard.

When Princeton coach Bob Surace had to inform them that the doctors had decided Travis needed another week after, I pointed out to one of them that it was a long way to come to *not* see Travis play. The scout shrugged. "Harvard's got some players on defense worth seeing," he said. "And you never know when you're going to see someone you didn't know about."

People often ask me after I finish a book if anything surprised me. In the case of this book, the answer is emphatically yes and emphatically no.

The no was with the kind of people I met—on and off the field. I expected them to be bright and thoughtful, and they were all of that. The coaches gave me complete access from day one, not only in terms of the time I needed with the players but also my access on game days.

As for the yes, I never dreamed there would be so much turnover in the coaching ranks during 2023. It started with Buddy Teevens's horrific and ultimately fatal bicycle-riding accident in March. Then Al Bagnoli retired in early August and was replaced on interim basis by Mark Fabish, who was replaced shortly after the season ended by Jon Poppe. Cornell's David Archer, who like Fabish was told before his last game that he was going to be fired after ten years on the job, was replaced by Penn's offensive coordinator, Dan Swanstrom. And, on January 17, 2024, Harvard's Tim Murphy retired after thirty seasons at the school and an Ivy League record two hundred wins. Four weeks later, Harvard surprised most of the football world (and Harvard world) by naming Princeton graduate Anthony Aurich to replace Murphy. In what felt like an instant, Harvard went from someone with thirty-six years of head coaching experience to someone with zero years of head coaching experience—another complaint made by many Harvard alums.

They were entitled to be a bit spoiled in this area. Since the departure of Lloyd Jordan at the end of the Ivy League's first official season (1956), three men had been the head football coach—John Yovicsin for twelve years, Joe Restic for twenty-two years, and Murphy for thirty years. That's three coaches in sixty-four years. It's worth noting that Yovicsin had been the head coach at D-3 Gettysburg before coming to Harvard, and Restic had no head coaching experience before beginning his run at Harvard. Yale's Carm Cozza was a head coach for thirty-one years, all of them at Yale.

All of this means that there will be three new coaches when the 2024 season begins and one second-year coach, Dartmouth's Sammy McCorkle, who began last season as the "acting head coach" and ended it as the league's Coach of the Year after taking his team to an unlikely share of the conference title.

The turnover in coaches was certainly a surprise given the league's history of coaching stability. Teevens was a tragedy nobody could have foreseen. Bagnoli's retirement surprised everyone—including his team—even though he had just turned seventy. He looked completely healthy during spring practice, but the heart procedure he'd had in March had taken more out of him than he had thought it would and the thought of another season—his thirty-first—going through the intensity of a condensed but intense Ivy League schedule was ultimately something he decided he wasn't capable of going through.

"First time in forty years I've had Labor Day weekend off," he said at Columbia's opening game at Lafayette. "It was amazing how much I enjoyed it."

Bagnoli knew in June that he didn't have the stamina—physically or emotionally—to coach another season, but he didn't announce his retirement until August 4 because he wanted to be sure that Fabish would be named the interim coach and there would be no changes on the rest of the staff because the season was only six weeks away.

As it turned out, that was a good news/bad news decision for Fabish.

"I understood why Al did it and I'm grateful he made sure I got a chance," he said. "But it was a lot to handle going from assistant coach to head coach at that time of year. Everyone had to take on a different role. The players were used to Al's being the most important voice in the room. Ultimately, all of us were at Columbia because of him.

"It's to the credit of the kids that they bought in to everything we were trying to accomplish. Unfortunately, that didn't show up often enough when it came to wins and losses.

"I would have loved to have had a full year, starting with offseason workouts to spring practice and then to preseason and the season itself. That part was disappointing. I was judged on our record. That's disappointing too, but I understand that's the way it is."

Most Ivy League coaches get more than one year to establish a program and their own culture—culture perhaps being the most overused word in sports. Every new coach talks about the culture he wants to create when he takes a job. In college sports, a "culture" is established when better players are recruited.

Bagnoli's last Columbia team went 6–4 in 2022. The 2023 team had an excellent defense but lacked a consistent quarterback in a league with very good quarterbacks, ones who made plays late in close games.

"Harvard and Yale were better than us," Fabish said. "We could have beaten the other five Ivy League teams and came close in all those games. But close doesn't count."

If his players had a vote, Fabish would still be coaching at Columbia.

"I loved playing for Coach Bagnoli," Mason Tomlin said. "But I also loved playing for Coach Fab. Both terrific coaches and better men."

David Archer was also judged—after ten years—on his won-lost record. He certainly wasn't judged on his character or his work ethic or on how his players felt about him. If he had been, he would have been named coach for life.

And yet, Archer was surprised and disappointed when Cornell athletic director Nicki Moore told him she was making a change. The surprise was that this news came a week after Moore had told him she thought Cornell would be taking a step back if she fired him. The disappointment was feeling like the program was close to getting over the hump even though he didn't have the record to prove it. His players had the same feeling.

"We started out hot," quarterback Jameson Wang said. "I mean we beat Yale at Yale—that certainly wasn't supposed to happen. But, looking back, as much as the *win* was important, it was also very costly."

Cornell suffered several losses to injury during the game but the most important, by far, was team captain Jake Stebbins, who went down during the Yale game with what was, in essence, a season-ending knee injury.

Stebbins had decided to come back for a fifth COVID season in the locker room moments after Cornell's loss in the 2022 finale at Columbia had denied the Big Red their first winning season since 2005. "I just knew I didn't want it to end that way," he said before the 2023 season began. "I knew better things were ahead."

Like any Ivy Leaguer who returns for a fifth season, Stebbins had to drop out of school for the spring semester so he would still be an undergraduate in the fall. Cornell opened with a win on the road at Lehigh followed by the stunning upset at Yale the following week.

"We were hot, we were playing the way we believed we could play," quarterback Jameson Wang said. "Even when we were down [14–0] at halftime, we knew we could come back and win the game."

Which they did, winning 23–21 on a field goal by place kicker/punter Jackson Kennedy as time expired. The Big Red had come back to lead 20–14, then fallen behind 21–20 late, before driving into range for Kennedy's third field goal in the dying seconds of the game.

But Stebbins's injury took a lot of the joy out of what was Cornell's biggest victory in years.

"When he went down, I could just tell he was badly hurt," Wang said. "My heart sank right there. It's almost impossible to describe how important Jake was to us, not just as a terrific linebacker. It went way beyond that. He was the heart and soul of the team for two years. He was our captain and our leader. Everyone looked up to Jake."

His teammates and coaches unanimously echoed Wang's sentiment. Clearly something went out of the team when Stebbins went down. It wasn't just missing their best player on defense, it was missing his voice on the practice field every day and in the locker room.

"Look, injuries are a part of football," Archer said. "Every coach can look back on a season and explain how injuries hurt his team. I've never believed in making excuses, especially those associated with injuries. The best teams are the ones that overcome injuries.

"But there are injuries and there are *injuries*. Losing Jake was huge. It didn't mean we couldn't win games, it just made everything harder for all of us. And it took a lot out of winning at Yale for us. Don't get me wrong, it was a big deal, but losing Jake was emotionally painful for all of us."

Wang knew that Stebbins's injury was going to be difficult to overcome but still believed his team had the players to have a good season.

"The Bucknell game was the one that really hurt, I think," he said. "Losing to Colgate the week after we beat Yale was disappointing, but they had a good team. I just didn't think Bucknell was very good [the Bison finished 4–7]. They didn't do anything that impressed me—except beat us."

Cornell did bounce back to beat Brown the last Saturday in October and went into Franklin Field on the first Saturday in November tied for third place in the league with a 2–2 record—the same as everyone else in the league except for Harvard and Princeton, each 3–1, and Columbia, which was 0–4.

"The fact is, we went into November with a chance to win a title," Wang said. "That hasn't happened around here in a *long* time. That was good but Penn beat us soundly, especially in the first half [the Quakers led 16–0 at the break]. That was bad."

Cornell then lost its last two games to Dartmouth and Columbia and several players—Wang among them—admitted a lot went out of them after the Penn loss. "We went into the season thinking we were good enough to win the league," Wang said. "After the Penn game, we knew that dream was gone. We were done. That was tough to get over."

Harvard's dream was to win the league outright. The players wondered if their coach might retire at the end of the season but managed to keep their focus on ending their six-season drought without an Ivy League title.

"We didn't really have expectations going into the season," said running back Shane McLaughlin, who became the first offensive player elected captain at the 2023 postseason banquet since Ryan Fitzpatrick in 2004. "We'd lost a lot of guys to graduation—both quarterbacks, starting running backs, the entire secondary. Our motto was to go out every day—practice and games—and be young and hungry.

"Then we started 5–0 and beat Holy Cross. That was when we started to think we could go undefeated. We let Princeton slip through our fingers, and we lost a great game to Yale. But we still tied for the title and that was an accomplishment."

He smiled. "Winning outright would have been better but losing that game just fuels us for next season. I feel as if my captaincy has already started. I have had two great captains—Jordan Hill and Nate Leskovec—so I know what to do, or at least think I know what to do."

Although they had known it was possible, Murphy's retirement and Aurich's hiring shook the players. They all said the right things when Aurich was hired, but there was definitely unrest in the Harvard world after Aurich arrived.

"I think we all felt that Coach [Scott] Larkee should have been hired," said Leskovec, who, as a graduating senior, could speak freely. "We had a circle of the last four captains who tried to figure out how to influence the decision-makers into hiring Coach Larkee. I know Ms. McDermott [Harvard AD Erin] had more than a thousand letters supporting Coach Larkee, but in the end she and the committee chose Coach Aurich.

"We certainly weren't happy at the time, but now we have to give him a fair chance. I'll be at all the home games."

Harvard and Yale could both walk away from their seasons satisfied to know they had won another Ivy League title. But, like everyone else in the league, they would agree that the most remarkable story in the league was Dartmouth—for reasons both good and tragic.

Josh Balara's death due to adrenal cancer in March wasn't a surprise because the last time he'd been on campus in the fall, he had looked very sick and, deep down, everyone understood it was just a matter of time.

Even so, the players were still reeling when athletic director Mike Harrity asked them to an emergency Zoom meeting a couple of days later. Most were away from campus for spring break, which is why the meeting was done over Zoom.

"I think we all knew it had to be something very serious for Mr. Harrity to call a Zoom meeting that quickly during break," quarterback Nick Howard said. "When he told us about the accident and that Coach Mac was going to be acting coach, we knew it had to be pretty bad."

The players weren't told much during the next few months, but it was apparent that Teevens's injuries were critical. Led by the example of McCorkle and the coaching staff, the players kept "moving forward."

Teevens died on September 19, three days after an opening loss to a ranked New Hampshire team and four days prior to the home opener against Lehigh. After a rousing pregame speech by McCorkle in which he never for a moment talked about the game itself, the Big Green won easily, 34–17.

A week later, they stunned Penn at Franklin Field, which everyone agreed later was critical to their success. They were 3–4—but 2–2 in the league—when they played Princeton on the first Friday in November. Owen Zalc's third field goal of the night—from 47 yards—gave Dartmouth a thrilling 23–21 victory.

With fourth-and-two on the Princeton 30 yard line, McCorkle decided on going for the field goal.

Zalc, a five-foot-nine freshman from Cary, North Carolina, who had grown up a Duke fan, had been recruited early by several ACC schools and by South Carolina. But when his father, Eli, saw his junior board scores, he said, "You're applying to Ivy League schools." His SAT number was 1440; his ACT was 34; and, including AP classes, he had a 4.46 GPA.

Zalc visited several Ivy League schools but knew he had found a home when he visited Dartmouth. Plus, Teevens, who always coached the special teams, made him a priority recruit from the beginning.

"He called all the time," Zalc said. "Always talked about my parents and my sisters, who were runners. He was a big runner, so he understood them. I was so looking forward to playing for him."

Then came the accident. Zalc never got to kick for Teevens. But on that cold Friday night in November, McCorkle had faith in him to make the kick.

"I had already made four 47-yarders during the season," he said. "I knew I could make it, and so did Coach Mac."

He drilled the kick with 1:54 left and shook a fist—once—a rare act of celebration. "Actually, I started thinking right away, 'I need a good kickoff, there's lots of time left,'" he said. "I was about as proud of the kickoff as the field goal."

The Dartmouth defense stopped the Princeton offense and the Big Green stayed alive in the Ivy League race. Easy victories over Cornell and Brown the next two weeks and Yale's victory over Harvard landed them at 5–2 and tied for first place—an outcome that bordered on miraculous to say the least.

"It feels to me like every Ivy League season is remarkable," Jack Ford said. "But this one went way beyond that. This one was extraordinary."

I would certainly agree with that assessment. I loved every second I spent on the eight campuses—not so much the hours on I-95—and came away respecting the players and coaches almost unanimously.

The Dartmouth-Brown game ended eleven minutes before The Game ended. When McCorkle told the players and families to wait on the field for the game to end, a multi-phone watch party broke out. When the final score came in, cheering and hugs took over the field. Along with a lot of tears.

"I think we were all thinking about Buddy," McCorkle said. "We knew he was enjoying the whole thing with us."

I never did get to see Buddy Teevens coach in 2023, but we talked at length about the project in late February. The next day, I received a text from him.

It said: "So excited that you're going to do this book. Can't wait to finally get you up here to Dartmouth. We will do everything we can to help you. Can't wait to get started. Thanks for wanting to do this. You will love the kids at all eight schools . . . Buddy."

As usual, he had it right. I loved the kids and the coaches. I loved finally getting to experience Dartmouth. And I loved the story the Dartmouth football team and the rest of The Ancient Eight allowed me to tell.

# ACKNOWLEDGMENTS

I'm never quite sure where to begin acknowledgments because so many people are needed to help me put a book together.

*The Ancient Eight* is no exception to that rule.

I interviewed eighty-two players, and I can honestly say I enjoyed each of them. All the coaches—the bosses and their assistants—were remarkably patient with me. Several others went out of their way to make the logistics of the project as easy as possible for me. As usual, my friends and family were there to take me to the finish line.

I guess the place to begin is with the eight coaches who were in charge during the 2023 season. I'll go in the order of the final standings: Tim Murphy at Harvard; Tony Reno at Yale; Sammy McCorkle at Dartmouth (all three tied for first place); Bob Surace at Princeton; Ray Priore at Pennsylvania; James Perry at Brown; Dave Archer at Cornell; and Mark Fabish at Columbia.

Al Bagnoli was still coaching at Columbia when I started the project and Jon Poppe had taken over there by the time I finished. Dan Swanstrom was Penn's offensive coordinator at the start of the season and then succeeded Archer at Cornell. Andrew Aurich stepped into huge shoes when he became Harvard's coach after Murphy retired this past January.

Special thanks to Princeton associate head coach Steve Verbit, who not only guided me in the right direction throughout the season but was my informal historian, having been at Princeton since 1986.

Last among the coaches—but certainly not least—is Buddy Teevens. He never got to coach a game during my research but played a critical role in my writing the book. He and Murphy—best friends since boyhood—were the first two people I called when I had the idea to try to do this. Both were encouraging and pledged complete cooperation—Tim in his low-key way; Buddy in his all-exclamation-points way. I still remember him saying, "This is going to be so great!" during our first phone conversation.

He was, of course, right—it was a great experience for me. I can't possibly list everyone who helped me with logistics, but a few stand out: Jackson McSherry at Harvard; Alex Peffley at Cornell; Mike Kowalsky at Columbia; Warren Croxton and Jerry Price at Princeton; Tim Bennett at Yale; Josh Liddick at Penn; and the amazingly patient Dino Cauteruccio Jr. at Dartmouth; and Dartmouth undergraduate journalist Will Dehmel.

There is no way for me to adequately thank all the players for their time. Some didn't even make the book because I was in the lucky position of having too much information and too many stories to tell. I apologize to them.

There were also those who played important roles in the book and kept responding to my follow-up requests for more time. Among them: Harvard's Nate Leskovec, Shane McLaughlin, Jake Rizy, Charles DePrima, Logan Bednar, Cooper Barkate, Matt Hudson, and Tyler Neville; Yale's Wande Owens, Nolan Grooms, and Ezekiel Larry; Dartmouth's Nick Howard, Owen Zalc, Josh Green, Joshua and Jabari Johnson, and Grayson O'Bara; Princeton's Jalen Travis, Blake Stenstrom, Ozzie Nicholas, Liam Johnson, Luke Colella, John Volker, Matthew Mahoney, and Connor Hulstein;

Columbia's Mason Tomlin, Caden Bell, and Josh Giorgi; Cornell's Jameson Wang, Jake Stebbins, Micah Sahakian, Jackson Kennedy, and Nicholas Laboy; Penn's Joey Slackman, Aidan Sayin, Graham Gotlieb; Mohamed Diakite, Jake Bingham, Jake Peterson, Aaron Jones, and Sean Williams; and Brown's Jake Willcox, Wes Rockett, Ethan Royer, Stockton Owen, Kyle Philbin, Mark Mahoney, and Isaiah Reed.

This book doesn't happen without the encouragement and enthusiasm of Brant Rumble, my editor at HBGUSA, and without the support of my agent, Andrew Blauner. Michael Pietsch and I first worked together in 1994 on *A Good Walk Spoiled*, and it was Michael who took me on when he was the boss at HBGUSA when most publishers were afraid of *Take a Fist, Raise a Knee.* His importance in my career—and as a friend—can't possibly be overstated.

Then there are the usual suspects in my life: Keith and Barbie Drum, Jackson Diehl, Jean Halperin, Tate Armstrong, Sally Jenkins, Andy Dolich, Terry Hanson, David and Linda Maraniss, Bob Woodward, Elsa Walsh, Jim Cantelupe, Derek Klein, Tim Kelly, Dick Hall, Bob Beretta, Ken Niumatalolo, Eric Ruden, Chet Gladchuk, Scott Strasemeier; Courtney Holt, Bob Matte, Dick (Hoops) and Joanie Weiss, and the Red Auerbach lunch group that continues on: Aubre Jones, Murray Lieberman, (Uncle) Lew Flashenberg; Mark Hughes, Craig Berrington, Steve Polakoff, Geoff Kaplan, Stanley Copeland, Jeff Gemunder, Joe McKeown, Bob Campbell, Pete Dowling, and Harry Huang.

Also: Mike Wilbon, Tony Kornheiser, Lesley Visser, Paul Goydos, David and Joan Fay, Tom Watson, Chris Ryan, Tommy Amaker, Gary Williams, Mike Krzyzewski, Griff Aldrich, Ryan Odom, Andrew Bogusch, and Linda Falkerson. My editors and colleagues at *The Washington Post*: Dan Steinberg, Jason Murray, Matt Rennie, Gene Wang, Mark Maske, and, in absentia, the great Don Graham.

Last, never least, my family. My three children: Danny, Brigid, and Jane, who is fourteen going on twenty-four. My two ex-wives—the mothers of those children: Mary and Christine. Margaret, my sister, and Bobby, my brother. Both have been there to help me through tough times. My first book editor, Jeff Neuman, counseled me years ago to NOT mention my cats. He wasn't wrong. But this is my fiftieth book, so the hell with it. I miss Alan and I miss Mia and all those who went before. Anyone wants to criticize me for that—fine.

Never did I dream I'd write fifty books. I can honestly say number fifty was as much fun as I've ever had. For that, I am truly grateful to everyone involved.

—John Feinstein,
May 6, 2024,
Potomac, Maryland

# INDEX